Christ Our Companion

Christ Our Companion

Toward a Theological Aesthetics of Liberation

Roberto S. Goizueta

ORBIS BOOKS

Maryknoll, New York 10545

Founded in 1970, Orbis Books endeavors to publish works that enlighten the mind, nourish the spirit, and challenge the conscience. The publishing arm of the Maryknoll Fathers and Brothers, Orbis seeks to explore the global dimensions of the Christian faith and mission, to invite dialogue with diverse cultures and religious traditions, and to serve the cause of reconciliation and peace. The books published reflect the opinions of their authors and are not meant to represent the official position of the Maryknoll Society. To obtain more information about Maryknoll and Orbis Books, please visit our website at www.maryknollsociety.org.

Georges Rouault, French, 1871-1958, *Christ and Disciples, plate fifteen from the Passion*, 1936; published 1939. Color aquatint on tan laid paper, 300 x 213 mm (image); 308 x 220 mm (plate); 446 x 341 mm (sheet). Gift in memory of Kay Goodman King from the A. Peter Dewey Memorial Fund, 1946.66.15, The Art Institute of Chicago. Photography © The Art Institute of Chicago. Art © 2009 Artists Rights Society (ARS), New York / ADAGP, Paris.

Manufactured in the United States of America.

Library of Congress Cataloging-in-Publication Data

Goizueta, Roberto S.
    Christ our companion : toward a theological aesthetics of liberation / Roberto S. Goizueta.
      p. cm.
    Includes index.
    ISBN 978-1-57075-853-9 (pbk.)
    1. Spirituality—Catholic Church. 2. Christian life—Catholic authors. 3. Hispanic American Catholics. 4. Hispanic Americans—Religion. 5. Hispanic American theology. 6. Catholic Church—Doctrines. 7. Aesthetics—Religious aspects—Christianity. I. Title.
  BX1407.H55G66 2009
  248.2089'68—dc22

                       2009011020

To my wife, Elizabeth

Contents

Preface

Several years ago I was giving a talk at a poor, inner-city Latino/a parish in Chicago. At one point in my presentation on the Gospels, I inadvertently lapsed into academic-speak and referred to these texts as "narratives." Immediately, a hand went up among the group gathered in the parish hall. An obviously perturbed middle-aged man, who had identified himself as Jesús, yelled out impatiently, "They're not 'narratives.' They're the *Gospels*!"

This and similar experiences I've had since then have challenged me to reexamine presuppositions and assumptions that I've harbored concerning what we scholars can so easily describe as the "faith of the people" or "popular Catholicism." The people themselves continually challenge me to question the unspoken assumptions that underlie my academic training and professional context. What was Jesús trying to suggest? That, maybe, the Gospels are more than just narratives? And what assumptions were latent in my use of the term "narrative"—assumptions that he had perceived and to which I had been insensitive?

What I've since come to realize is that the question posed to me that day was none other than the question which that *other* Jesus had posed to Peter, "Who do you say that I am?" I felt as convicted as Peter must have felt. Like so many other times over the years, at that moment I had a profound, in-your-face experience of what we theologians call the epistemological privilege of the poor.

These experiences have led me not only to reexamine my own intellectual assumptions but also to reread other theological texts in the light of the experiences. How might Jesús respond, for example, to the writings of formative figures in my own intellectual training such as Gustavo Gutiérrez and Jon Sobrino? Would they be susceptible to similar challenges? It became evident to me that, in fact, Jesús would not have reacted to them as he had reacted to me; they would have been clearer, more up front about what they believed.

The following pages are the product of my own struggle to come to grips theologically and spiritually with the faith of Jesús, the faith of many others like him who have crossed my path, and the challenge that their deep faith represents for my own. On the way, I've discovered new dimensions in the thought of other old companions like Sobrino, Virgilio Elizondo, Enrique Dussel, and many others. I've also discovered new interlocutors, sometimes in unexpected places, among scholars whom I might earlier have dismissed precisely because of my own unexamined assumptions about their work.

One such theologian was Hans Urs von Balthasar. For years, I'd had serious concerns about his work, especially because it had been used to support a neoconservative social agenda with which I was often in serious disagreement. Yet, as happened with my new reading of Latin American liberation theologians, as I reread Balthasar's theological aesthetics I began to discover insights that challenged me in much the same way that Jesús in Chicago had challenged me. I harbored significant misgivings about Balthasar's theology—and still do.[1] My concern in the following pages, however, is not to present a thorough, systematic critique of Balthasar or, for that matter, of Gutiérrez, Sobrino, other liberation theologians, or U.S. Latino and Latina theologians. Rather I draw on some fundamental insights that, I believe, these theologians have in common, even if often articulated with quite different emphases. I also found in Balthasar an underlying theological method that, though with a different focus, has much in common with the Latin American and U.S. Hispanic theologies I've been reading for so long.

If there is one statement that encapsulates this similarity, it is the Johannine assertion that "God loved us first." Theologians like Gutiérrez, Sobrino, and Elizondo have made crucial contributions to our understanding of that statement. In the following pages I suggest that those contributions, while perhaps not fully appreciated by theologians such as Balthasar himself, are not inconsistent with the Swiss theologian's fundamental insights concerning the foundational priority of God's love. The following pages represent, then, my own halting and ongoing attempt to unpack the implications of the inspiring yet demanding statement, "God loved us first."

Acknowledgments

Some material in this book has previously appeared elsewhere, often in different form and in earlier versions, including the following publications: "Challenges of/to the U.S. Latino/a Liturgical Community," *Liturgical Ministry* 16 (Summer 2007): 124-131; "*Corpus Verum*: Toward a Borderland Ecclesiology," *Journal of Hispanic/Latino Theology* online (December 2007), http://latinotheology.com/2007/borderland_ecclesiology; "'Put Your Finger Here . . .': Reconciliation and the Refusal to Cease Suffering," The Msgr. Philip J. Murnion Lecture of the Catholic Common Ground Initiative (New York: National Pastoral Life Center, 2006); "The Crucified and Risen Christ: From Calvary to Galilee," Presidential Address, in *Proceedings of the Catholic Theological Society of America* 60 (2005): 57-71; "Because God Is Near, God Is Real," in Peter Horsfield, Mary Hess, and Adán Medrano, eds., *Belief in Media: Cultural Perspectives on Media and Christianity* (London: Ashgate, 2004); "The Symbolic Realism of U.S. Latino/a Popular Catholicism," *Theological Studies* 65, no. 2 (June 2004): 255-274; "Knowing the God of the Poor: The Preferential Option for the Poor," in *Opting for the Margins: Postmodernity and Liberation in Christian Theology*, ed. Joerg Rieger (New York: Oxford University Press, 2003), 143-156; "The Symbolic World of Mexican American Religion," in *Horizons of the Sacred: Mexican Traditions in U.S. Catholicism*, ed. Timothy Matovina and Gary Riebe-Estrella (Ithaca, N.Y., and London: Cornell University Press, 2002), 119-138; "A Christology for a Global Church," in *Beyond Borders: Writings of Virgilio Elizondo and Friends*, ed. Timothy Matovina (Maryknoll, N.Y.: Orbis Books, 2000), 150-158; "A *Ressourcement* from the Margins: U.S. Latino Popular Catholicism as Lived Religion," in *Theology and Lived Christianity*, ed. David M. Hammond (Mystic, Conn.:

Twenty-Third Publications, 2000), 3-37; "Locating the Absolutely Absolute Other: Toward a Transmodern Christianity," in *Thinking from the Underside of History: Enrique Dussel's Philosophy of Liberation*, ed. Linda Martín Alcoff and Eduardo Mendieta (Lanham, Md.: Rowman and Littlefield Publishers, 2000), 181-193; "'There You Will See Him': Christianity beyond the Frontier Myth," in *The Church as Counterculture*, ed. Michael Budde and Robert Brimlow (Albany, N.Y.: SUNY Press, 2000), 171-193; "Making Christ Credible: U.S. Latino/a Popular Catholicism and the Liberating Nearness of God," in *Practicing Catholic: Ritual, Body, and Contestation in Catholic Faith*, edited by Bruce T. Morrill, Susan Rodgers, Joanna E. Ziegler (New York: Palgrave Macmillan, 2006), 169-178.

1

Proclaiming the Truth of Christ
in the Twenty-First Century

The claim that Jesus Christ is the "Way, the Truth, and the Life" is today more incredible than ever. In a world rent by violence and division of every stripe, where the very possibility that life may indeed be worth living can so often seem illusory, the message of Christ's life, death, and resurrection appears as a pipe dream at best and a cruel hoax at worst. At the same time, an increased consciousness of the amazingly diverse, pluralistic world in which we all live raises important questions about the ethical and theological defensibility of any religious position—particularly when the rationale for so much of the violence we see around us is ostensibly grounded precisely in religious principles. In such a world, how can a Christian proclaim that message credibly and responsibly? How can one speak of Jesus Christ in the wake of the events of September 11, 2001?

My conviction is that the answer to this question can only be discovered as we, through our everyday actions, respond to Christ's claim to be the Way, the Truth, and the Life by embodying that claim in our actions. The truth of which Christ speaks and which he is, is a lived truth. This assertion is hardly new, since it has been at the heart of Christian belief from the beginning: ultimately, the credibility of Christ's claims rests on the evidence presented by those persons who have lived out those claims, the "cloud of witnesses" whose lives testify to the transformative power of the crucified and risen One. For the contemporary Christian struggling to find some way of remaining true to his or her experience of God as revealed in the person of Jesus Christ while remaining true to his or her experience of the universality of God's love, there is an alternative: the lived faith of those who are participants in Christ's ongoing work.

The most convincing testament to the truth of the Christian faith are the persons whose everyday lives have embodied that faith, from the time of Christ to the present—not just those saints officially recognized by the church through its canonization process, but the millions more who toil in the obscurity of their homes, neighborhoods, and communities. Each of us knows who these holy ones are, for they have touched our lives, befriended us, nurtured us, challenged us, inspired us. More than any abstract principle, dogma, or theological proposition, the concrete lives of these exemplary Christians are what have attracted us to Christ. Their lives and testimonies witness to the credibility of the Christian kerygma. Pope John Paul II often spoke of the central significance of these holy persons in the life and mission of the church:

> One fruit of the conversion brought about by the Gospel is the *holiness* of so many men and women in our time: not only those whom the Church has officially proclaimed saints, but all those who with simplicity and amid the circumstances of their daily lives testified to their fidelity to Christ. How can one not think of the countless sons and daughters of the Church who throughout . . . history have lived lives of generous and authentic holiness in the hiddenness of their family and their professional and social lives? . . . The Lord Jesus promised: "He who believes in me will also do the works that I do; and greater works than these will he do, because I go to the Father" (*Jn* 14:12). The saints are living proof of the fulfillment of this promise, and they encourage the belief that this is possible in the most difficult hours of history.[1]

Drawing on the earliest Christian traditions, moreover, John Paul II repeatedly called on us to look to the long line of Christian martyrs for the paradigmatic examples of lived Christian faith and the most convincing argument for its credibility:

The martyrs know that they have found the truth about life in the encounter with Jesus Christ, and nothing and no-one could ever take this certainty from them. Neither suffering nor violent death could ever lead them to abandon the truth which they have discovered in the encounter with Christ. This is why to this day the witness of the martyrs continues to arouse such interest, to draw agreement, to win such a hearing and to invite emulation. This is why their word inspires such confidence: from the moment they speak to us of what we perceive deep down as the truth we have sought for so long, the martyrs provide evidence of a love that has no need of lengthy arguments in order to convince. The martyrs stir in us a profound trust because they give voice to what we already feel and they declare what we would like to have the strength to express.[2]

If we are drawn to Christ, therefore, it will likely not be because we have been convinced by theological arguments, but because we have been inspired by the witness of his martyrs and saints. "From the hope of these people who have been touched by Christ," suggests Pope Benedict XVI, "hope has arisen for others who were living in darkness and without hope."[3] In the final analysis, it is not the rationality of theological arguments that will convince us of the truth of the Christian faith, but the beauty of those lives in which that faith is incarnated and made visible and palpable. As the Uruguayan theologian Juan Luis Segundo has argued, at the most fundamental level, human beings are attracted not to beliefs and values in the abstract but to particular persons, particular lives—and, because we are attracted to these particular persons, we are attracted to the beliefs and values they hold.[4]

My own life has been forever changed by the holy lives that Christ used to draw and attract me to him. As with so many Latinos and Latinas, for example, my *abuelita* (grandmother) was the spiritual heart of my family. What I remember most about her—even several years after her death—was her absolute confidence in God. One of her favorite sayings was, "*Me conformo.*" While there is no exact English translation of that phrase, and the closest translation would be "I adapt myself," the literal translation is, of course, "I conform." "I conform" to whatever God has in store for me; I will allow myself to be formed by God's will. And she did—through the tumultuous years of exile from her native country, with all the personal, familial, and material upheaval that brought. Hers was by no means a passive adaptation, since it demanded constant struggle to hold together a family that had been devastated by the experience of revolution and exile to a foreign land. My admiration for her drew me to Christ by making me desire to conform to her God, a God in whom one could confide completely, come what may.

While the holy persons in our lives are often found in our families, sometimes we encounter them only in passing, as momentary blessings who nevertheless have a lasting impact on our own lives. I had one such encounter many years ago, while I was in college. The school's campus was in an urban setting, surrounded by very poor neighborhoods. The sight of homeless persons asking for spare change was a common one on the streets immediately surrounding the campus. Walking those streets at night in search of a sandwich at a local restaurant or a movie at a cinema, I would regularly come across a homeless man or woman, reach into my pocket, and place a couple of coins in his or her hand. It made me feel good. One particular evening, I happened upon a stocky, scruffy-looking, middle-aged homeless man standing on a street corner. As I approached him, he looked at me straight in the eye and asked for money. Perfunctorily, I reached into my pants pocket for loose change and placed the coins in his hand. After putting the money away, he came toward me with both arms outstretched and reached to grab my head. My heart stopped. As an enlightened, college-educated young man with the self-assurance such young men so often have, I had always assumed I had risen above any petty bigotry or prejudices I may have harbored as a child. Yet at this moment I became numb with fear, fully expecting that I was about to be mugged. The scruffy homeless man did indeed grab my head. He put both hands on my forehead, as if to extend a blessing, and said calmly, "Thank you. God bless you."

I walked away in a daze, trying to process what had just transpired, both the man's actions and my own instinctive reaction. I had a profound sense of both gratitude and shame. By the time I had composed myself and returned to the street corner to thank him for what he had done for me, he was already gone. For weeks after that, I returned to that street corner hoping to see him so that I could thank him. I never saw him again.

This event was hardly earth shattering or history making, yet it did shatter my life. My world with its preconceptions was turned upside down. In the man's outstretched arms, I was confronted by a love that manifested itself where I least expected to find it; indeed, I had been under the assumption that it was I who, through my charity, was bringing God's love to this homeless man. His "God bless you" in the face of my fear confronted me like a mirror that revealed an ugly reality: my own prejudices. This poor, homeless man was but one of millions of similar persons, the vast majority forgotten by history, whose lives have borne witness to a love that irrupts in our worlds and shatters them forever, a love that transforms hearts of stone, turning them into hearts of flesh and blood. From then on, I've desired nothing more than to believe—*really* believe—and come to know the same God whom that homeless man clearly knew so intimately. I gave the man a few cents; he gave me faith in the power of God's grace to challenge and transform my heart . . . and through nothing more dramatic than a softly spoken "God bless you."

It is to the lives of people like my *abuelita* and this homeless man that Christian theology must first look if it is to be credible in this violent, divided world of the twenty-first century. Neither of these were individuals reluctant to make truth claims or to make an explicit show of their faith, yet their concrete actions demonstrated that, far from foreclosing an openness to other persons, the truth that they asserted demanded such openness: "*Me conformo*," "God bless you." We Christian theologians could do a lot worse than to ground our theological reflections in those two phrases, and in the lived faith in which they were rooted.

Among contemporary theologies, two stand out as particularly influential attempts to retrieve the significance of lived faith for Christian theology: theological aesthetics and liberation theology. Both of these theological movements have insisted on the foundational importance of Christian praxis for Christian theology; theology is incomprehensible, meaningless, irrelevant, and false unless it is grounded in and oriented toward Christian discipleship. For both theological aesthetics and liberation theology, belief in

Jesus Christ is not so much a matter of creedal profession as a matter of personal conversion and practical conviction (though these always remain inextricably related).

At the same time, however, liberation theology has made a fundamental contribution to our understanding of what constitutes lived faith and who are the saints, the holy ones who reveal the truth of Christian faith. From its very beginnings, Christianity has looked to the saints and martyrs as the living paradigms of Christian faith, as those persons whose very lives (and deaths) represent the most convincing apologia for the faith. With their emphasis on praxis as the ground and goal of theology, liberation theologians are located squarely within that tradition, which looks to the lived faith as *locus theologicus*. Yet liberation theologians also call our attention in a special way to a particular dimension of the communion of saints, namely, the special place occupied by the poor and marginalized as privileged witnesses to the truth of Christ. Without idealizing or romanticizing the poor, who as a group are as prone to sin as any other group of human beings, liberation theology nevertheless emphasizes the theological significance of their lived faith in the midst of innocent suffering as a place where we encounter the power, the attractiveness, the beauty of Christ's truth. This is what Jon Sobrino calls "primordial saintliness":

> Saintliness does not have to be accompanied by heroic virtues—which are required for canonization; it is also expressed in a life of everyday heroism. We don't know whether these poor who cry out to live are saints-intercessors or not, but they have the power to move our hearts. They do not perform "miracles," in the sense of violating the laws of nature, which is also required for canonization. But it is not rhetorical to say that their miracles violate the laws of history; it is a miracle to survive in a hostile world that makes their life exceedingly hard. What we call primordial saintliness is the will to live and to survive amid great suffering, the decision and effort that it requires, the unlimited creativity, the strength, the constancy, defying innumerable problems and obstacles.[5]

In this book, I suggest that, as Christian theologians retrieve the significance of lived faith for theology, the lived faith of the primordial saints in our communities can be a source for understanding the intimate relationship between a theological aesthetics and a theology of liberation (*pace* those proponents of both who would see them as mutually opposed). Perhaps ironically, the reconciling truth of the crucified and risen Christ is revealed, above all, in the invincible faith of the victims of history, in their stubborn insistence that, in the face of all the evidence, life is worth living; life is a gift. If the young Guatemalan mother forced to decide which of her children will go without food today, because there is not enough for all, can still proclaim "*Caminemos con Jesús*" (We walk with Jesus), we must listen. If the elderly Cuban American woman whose family has been ravaged by the violence of exile can still kneel at the foot of the cross, we must pay attention. If the Mexican American farm worker lying in a hospital bed, suffering from a terminal illness caused by repeated exposure to toxic pesticides, can still lovingly caress the medals of *La Morenita* (affectionate term for the dark-skinned Virgin) and the *Sagrado Corazón* (the Sacred Heart) pinned to his pillow, we must not turn away. If it can honestly be affirmed at all, the absolute value of life as a gift will be affirmed most convincingly in the enduring faith, the hope against hope, of those persons who daily live at the very limits of life, at death's door. Paradoxically, it is the unloved, the despised of our world whom God has chosen to bring the good news to a world desperate to feel loved. That is the fundamental message of this book; it is, in my experience, the fundamental message of Jesus Christ.

CRISTO COMPAÑERO: CRUCIFIED AND RISEN

The refrain of one of the most popular and beautiful Latin American hymns declares: "Lord, you have looked into my eyes; smiling, you have called my name." That single line poignantly expresses the core Christian belief so prominent in the Gospels and especially in the writings of Paul: God loved us first. In a 1985 apostolic letter to the youth of the world, John Paul II speaks movingly of this "look of love" as the sum and substance of the Christian message:

> It is also my hope that, after you have made the discernment of the essential and important questions for you, for the plan of the whole life that lies before you, you will experience what the Gospel means when it says: "Jesus, looking upon him, loved him." May you experience a look like that! May you experience the truth that he, Christ, looks upon you with love! He looks with love upon every human being. The Gospel confirms this at every step. One can also say that this "loving look" of Christ contains, as it were, a summary and synthesis of the entire Good News. . . . My wish for each of you is that you may discover this look of Christ, and experience it in all its depth. . . . Man needs this loving look. He needs to know that he is loved, loved eternally and chosen from eternity. . . . When everything would make us doubt ourselves and the meaning of our life, then this look of Christ, the awareness of the love that in him has shown itself more powerful than any evil and destruction, this awareness enables us to survive. My wish for you then is that you may experience what the young man in the Gospel experienced: "Jesus, looking upon him, loved him."[6]

Before I look at Christ, Christ has already looked at me. Before I do, think, or feel anything, God has already lovingly looked into my eyes and, smiling, has called out my name. Every other article of Christian faith, every theological statement, is little more than a footnote to this central belief: my entire life is a *response* to a Lover whose very gaze and call have created me and named me, thereby compelling a response. Yet this is also the most unbelievable, literally in-credible aspect of Christian faith—except for those who, on the surface, would appear to have little reason to hold such a belief. As the Jesuit theologian Jon Sobrino observes, "The poor have no problems with God. The classic question of theodicy—the 'problem of God,' the atheism of protest—so reasonably posed by the nonpoor, is no problem at all for the poor (who in good logic ought of course to be the ones to pose it)."[7]

A great irony of our post-Enlightenment world is that the

rejection of God's love in the face of human suffering has come principally from those sectors of society most blessed by economic prosperity and material security. It is not the poor who have become secularized. Indeed, it was precisely their inattentiveness to the experience of the poor and marginalized that led the great modern prophets of "enlightenment" to fail in their annunciation of religion's demise. "It amuses me," wrote Ignacio Ellacuría not long before his death, "when people say 'God has disappeared from the world,' because God has disappeared from Europe or from the European universities; or that the world has entered a post-Christian age and I don't know what else. It's possible that here [in Europe], yes. But this is not the world."[8] Not only has religious faith not succumbed to the forces of secularization, but it continues to thrive and grow—particularly among the very peoples whose suffering is supposed to represent the most devastating argument against religious faith. Either the poor are horribly ignorant, infantile, manipulable, and untrustworthy, or else they're onto something. I prefer to believe that they're onto something.

And that something is the incredible though simple truth that life is worth living . . . no matter what. Again, paradoxically, the encounter with death, poverty, and human powerlessness in all its guises liberates us to fully embrace life itself. In the Christian tradition, this paradoxical liberation is expressed above all in the crucified and risen Christ. It is no accident, therefore, that the crucified Christ plays such a central role in Latino/a popular Catholicism.

Yet if the crucified Christ reveals that life is good no matter what, this life is no mere abstraction; it is life as defined and constituted by Love, that is, by relationships. However important are traditional interpretations of Christ's passion and death that focus on theological notions of atonement, redemption, or sacrifice, the fundamental practical significance of the Crucified is that, no matter what, God accompanies us. This is the sine qua non of all interpretations of the cross: if God is Love, then, like any true love, this Love desires to become completely one with the beloved, sharing with and accompanying the beloved in everything. Our own human experience of love bears this out; whether parent and child, husband and wife, or close friends, the lover desires to be totally one with the beloved, to share fully in the life of the beloved. Indeed, this desire becomes particularly acute precisely at those times when the beloved is undergoing struggle, pain, and suffering. At those times the father desires to take upon himself the pain of his prematurely terminally ill child, or the wife the pain of her laid-off husband, or the friend the struggles of his despondent friend. The incarnation and, especially, the passion and crucifixion of Christ are thus the manifestation of a Love that can only desire to share fully in our humanness, a Love that refuses to remain at arm's length in the face of human powerlessness and death.

The poor are the unlikely witnesses to the central claim of the Christian faith: "the Father loves you" (John 16:27). Not surprisingly, then, the Christ who accompanies us is at the heart of Latino/a popular Catholicism. For, as Hans Urs von Balthasar argues, "to say that God loves us would be an empty phrase—looking at the world as it is—had it not been substantiated by the Incarnation, Cross and Resurrection of Jesus, by his absolute solidarity with us and had it not involved a revelation of the innermost nature of God (Trinity as love) through Jesus' relationship with the Father in the Holy Spirit."[9] Christ is credible because he is with us, as is declared in this Peruvian song to "Nuestro Señor de los Milagros" (Our Lord of the Miracles):

> When the poor have nothing and yet share,
> When a man is thirsty and yet gives us water,
> When the weak person gives strength to a friend,
> It is God who walks in our steps.
>
> When joy grows and floods over us,
> When our lips proclaim the truth,
> When we love the simple person's feelings,
> It is God who walks in our steps.
>
> When the people organize and struggle together,
> When we conquer oppression with our struggles,
> When we establish justice for all,
> It is God who walks in our steps.[10]

This experience of God's presence with us, especially in our struggles, is what makes God's love believable, Christ's message credible, and life livable. "Be the problems of the 'truth' of Christ what they may," writes Sobrino, "his credibility is assured as far as the poor are concerned, for he maintained his nearness to them to the end. In this sense the cross of Jesus is seen as the paramount symbol of Jesus' approach to the poor, and hence the guarantee of his indisputable credibility."[11] Because Jesus accompanies us, he is real, and because he is real, he liberates. And the Cross is the guarantee that he does, in fact, remain with us—that he walks with us even today. Sobrino comments as follows:

> A vague, undifferentiated faith in God is not enough to gener-ate hope. Not even the admission that God is mighty, or that God has made promises, will do this. Something else besides the generic or abstract attributes of the divinity is necessary in order to generate hope. This distinct element—which, furthermore, is the fundamental characteristic of the Chris-tian God—is something the poor have discovered viscerally, and in reality itself: the nearness of God. God instills hope because God is credible, and God is credible because God is close to the poor. . . . Therefore when the poor hear and understand that God delivers up the Son, and that God is crucified—something that to the mind of the nonpoor will always be either a scandal or a pure anthropomorphism—then, paradoxically, their hope becomes real.[12]

God's nearness as symbolized by the Crucified is not the conse-quence of Christian belief so much as the foundation of belief. If asked to give a reason for our belief, we might repeat the words of the Mexican *abuelita* who, when asked to defend her devotion to Our Lady of Guadalupe, replied simply: "*Se quedó.*" She stayed. Guadalupe did not abandon us in our time of need but shared our pain with us, thus making it possible for us to struggle on.

The Crucified is not only a symbol of suffering but, even more, a symbol of indestructible hope, hope in a liberation experienced not first in some future victory but in the present, silent solidarity of the One who, like the Mother who accompanied him to Calvary, stays when everyone else has abandoned us. This hope born of compassion, or shared suffering, is beautifully conveyed in the verses of the Brazilian poet and Bishop Pedro Casaldáliga:

> Because your solitude is mine as well;
> And all of me is but a wound, where
> Some blood wells up; and where
> A dead man waits, I reclaim the spring,
> Dead with him already before my death.[13]

For those who have known such hope, "Perfect joy will not come at the hour of triumph; perfect joy was already experienced in the moment of silent obedience."[14] Silent obedience—like Christ on Calvary. Our silence meets God's silence. Yet the anguish of abandonment is experienced as painful only because it is experienced in its relationship to perfect joy, reconciliation, communion.

A WOUNDED RESURRECTION

In our journeying with *Cristo Compañero*, this Christ who accompanies us, the wounds "where some blood wells up" become the signs of that companionship and, therefore, the source of our hope. Yes, the resurrection will indeed ensure that our hope is not in vain, but not even the resurrection can erase the wounds; the resurrected, glorified body of Jesus Christ still bore (and bears) the wounds of companionship, compassion, solidarity . . . and betrayal and abandonment. The wounds on Christ's glorified body are the incarnated memory of the bonds that defined his life and death. Jesus' wounds are the direct, inevitable consequence of his compassionate relationships with the poor, sinners, prostitutes, and other presumed unsavory characters. The wounds are also the consequence of betrayed relationships, the betrayal Jesus suffered when his disciples abandoned him and fled out of fear for their own lives.

If it is truly the victory of life over death, then the resurrection must vindicate and restore not just the life of the individual person Jesus Christ; the resurrection must also vindicate and restore the relationships that themselves have helped define Christ. The resurrection must be more than the restoration to life of an autonomous, isolated individual; it must be the resurrection of *Cristo Compañero*, Christ-as-companion. The resurrection is the victory of companionship over abandonment, the victory of community over estrangement. Also resurrected are those bonds that had been severed at Calvary when Jesus' friends abandoned him. Without reconciliation there can be no resurrection.

Yet the troubling wounds remain, don't they? When the resurrected Christ appears to the cowering disciples, he shows them the wounds. Indeed, he demands that the disciples look at the wounds and insists, in the case of Thomas, that the unbelieving disciple put his hand in the wounds. What must have been an extraordinarily shocking, stomach-churning scene is powerfully depicted in the famous Caravaggio painting of Thomas peering curiously into the wound in Jesus' side, probing deep inside the open wound, his fingers peeling back folds of skin as if to examine just how deep the wound is. What must Thomas or any of the other disciples in the upper room have thought at the moment? What must have been running through their minds or, more importantly, through their hearts—they who, only three days earlier, had fled in terror from their friend as he was being dragged off to Calvary?

No wonder the disciples were frightened! Indeed, they must have been scared to death at the sight of the man they had just betrayed, who was now confronting them with the visible, concrete signs of that betrayal—those irksome wounds. The disciples had probably assumed that now that Jesus was dead, they could put the past behind them, chalk it up to a misguided idealism, and go on to live the lives of good, upstanding fishermen, tax collectors, and so on. But then Jesus walks in to remind them of that troubling past, to prick consciences that had just begun to find some equilibrium, however tenuous. Moreover, Jesus sticks his wounds in their faces. He doesn't say, "Let bygones be bygones" or "Forgive and forget." Instead, he refuses to allow his disciples to forget what they had done to him; Jesus forces them to confront the painful consequences of their abandonment and betrayal: "Look and see. . . . Put your hand here. . . . Do *not* forget what you have done to me!"

Before there can be a restoration of companionship, there must be a restoration of memory, the memory of innocent suffering. Far from implying a forgetting of past suffering, resurrection and reconciliation imply an acknowledgment that past injustices are never erased by future victories, past suffering remains forever a part of the history of the resurrection; the wounds remain forever inscribed on the body of Christ. The resurrected Christ is and will always be also the crucified Christ. Like Paul, Christians always preach a simultaneously crucified and risen Christ (not a once-crucified but now-risen Christ).

The restoration of the disciples' memory makes Jesus' approach even more in-credible. In the face of the disciples' betrayal and abandonment of Jesus, Jesus now approaches them with open arms, invites them to become reconciled, and sits down with them to break bread, to share a meal. The memory of innocent suffering, inscribed on the body of the resurrected Jesus, confronts the disciples not in order to condemn them but precisely to invite them to become reconciled, to invite them to participate in Jesus Christ's resurrection. Like the homeless man who confronted me many years ago, Jesus stretches out his arms not to denounce or attack but to bless. In the mirror that is Jesus' scarred body, the disciples see themselves convicted, challenged to repent, and invited to become reconciled.

An essential aspect of Christ's passion and crucifixion was his experience of abandonment; though the physical suffering he underwent was horrific enough, this itself must have paled in comparison to the profound emotional and spiritual suffering of experiencing himself abandoned by his closest friends and, above all, by God. If our own experiences of God's absence can bring such agony even though we have never known complete union with God, how utterly devastating must have been the experience of divine abandonment for Jesus, who had lived his entire life in perfect intimacy and union with God. However painful the physical torture he underwent, surely this spiritual torture made Christ's suffering on the cross the most horrific ever experienced. Many, many human beings have endured—and continue to endure— the physical pain that Jesus suffered, but no one has ever had to endure the extremity of his spiritual and emotional anguish. On the cross, God chooses to experience divine abandonment. In so doing, God chooses to embrace every form of human death, every human experience of abandonment, which, however terrifying, cannot ultimately compare to the terror experienced by Christ on the cross, where the Son himself cries out to his Father for help and hears only silence.

The resurrection would require and imply an affirmation of all those bonds in the face of death, Christ's bonds with the Father and with his disciples. If the resurrection affirms the Father's ultimate refusal to abandon the Son to the forces of death, so too does it call for a reconciliation that transforms Christ's estrangement from his disciples into a renewed community. When the resurrected Christ presents himself to the disciples, he thus invites them to believe not just that he himself has been raised from the dead but that a reconciled community of faith has now been made possible—if they will but acknowledge the enduring wounds and recognize themselves mirrored in those wounds, that is, if they accept Jesus' loving invitation to conversion.

THE DENIAL OF SUFFERING

The response to Christ's invitation—"put your fingers here . . . and believe"—defines Christian faith. Had Thomas recoiled from Christ's wounds in horror, the resurrected Christ could justifiably be identified with an unspoiled victory that overcomes death by obliterating it from our memory; this would truly be the conqueror Christ, "el Conquistador." The crucified and risen Christ embodies the intimate connection between death and life, the fact that woundedness is an integral dimension of all life, even if only as the ineradicable memory of suffering. To recoil from Christ's wound is to rupture that connection, to miss the very core of the Christian kerygma.

The refusal to face Christ's wounds, wounds that appear on his resurrected body, is *the* mortal sin (in the most literal sense of the term), for it leads inevitably to the death of others and, indeed, to our own death. Indeed, the murderous consequences of the denial of death in contemporary Western societies were examined in the 1970s by the social psychologist Ernest Becker, who argued that the anxiety and even terror that we experience in the face of our own mortality is the foundational experience around which we construct our selves and our societies.[15] This need to deny our mortality, our ultimate powerlessness in the face of death, is what drives us to construct personal identities, social institutions, ideologies, and belief systems that can make us feel invulnerable and ultimately invincible. To be a human being is to exist in a state of the most profound vulnerability and contingency; our lives are ultimately not in our control, for they can be extinguished at any moment. But we cannot bear this fact. So we construct a world that will shield us against this terrifying truth. Invariably, however, we eventually discover that the world we construct in order to shield us from our own mortality and powerlessness has resulted in the very opposite: a world that fosters death in all its forms. What Becker details is precisely the process by which the individual strives to exempt him- or herself from the common lot of all persons, our common mortality. That process ultimately deals death, to the others against whom the individual must assert his or her singular invulnerability, and death to the individual him- or herself, since the need to presume oneself invulnerable leads to total isolation—from other persons, from God, and even from oneself.

In the language of social psychology, Becker thus articulates the consequences of erasing, ignoring, or failing to acknowledge the wounds on the risen body of Christ—the consequences of interpreting the resurrection apart from its concrete history, which includes the abandonment signaled by the crowing cock as well as the wounds resulting from that abandonment. Those consequences are always horrific. The corollary of our obsessive need to feel invulnerable in the face of our mortality is the need to avoid all pain, all suffering, for these appear in our lives as unwanted reminders that we are not in control of our own lives, that we are indeed vulnerable. If death is the ultimate enemy, the ultimate threat to our sense of security and invulnerability, so too are all those partial deaths that foreshadow our common end: illness, old age, poverty, failure, abandonment—which must be avoided at all costs. Indeed, our consumer culture is premised upon and driven by the promise that all these forms of human vulnerability are avoidable . . . if we have a large enough bank account, the right kind of insurance, the latest model automobile, or the most effective deodorant ("Never let them see you sweat"). Likewise, authentic human relationships of mutual love and trust are to be shunned, since these always involve a dimension of vulnerability and even pain in the face of an other who, however much we may seek to control, always remains beyond our control; if one falls in love, one might get burned. So we surround ourselves with things that promise security and invulnerability, and we run from persons, since they demand vulnerability and the possibility of pain. We fall in love with cars, houses, mobile phones, and computers even as we remain unattached to human persons. (The global economic crisis of 2008-2009 has demonstrated the tenuousness of that love, yet it remains to be seen whether we have learned the lesson.)

But we run not just from any persons; rather, we run from weak, powerless, vulnerable, wounded persons in particular, for they especially threaten our sense of invulnerability. They are the mirrors of our own souls, whose very existence threatens our sense of invulnerability, security, and control. What I feared about that African American man who confronted me in inner-city New Haven was simply the fact that he was there, the fact that he confronted me and, in doing so, forced me to recognize my connection to him and to his predicament. That was terrifying.

In fact, the very existence of the wounded in our midst is so terrifying that we must eradicate them or, at least, hide them from view, get them off the streets—so that we won't have to see them and their uncomfortable wounds. So, argues Becker, the violence inflicted on the weak among us—from the Jews in Nazi concentration camps to the children left to die in the poverty of our contemporary concentration camps, the ghettoes of Western cities and third-world rural villages—is simply the social face of the denial of death. If we deny death, we inflict it, but we also inflict it on ourselves. The fear of pain and vulnerability that causes us to shun real human relationships, to shun that true love that always involves surrender and vulnerability in the face of an other, ultimately kills our interior life, our ability to feel anything—pain or joy or love. As psychologists remind us, if we repress painful feelings out of fear, we instinctively also repress any positive feelings; we cannot pick and choose which feelings to repress. To repress all feelings of insecurity or pain out of fear is to make joy and love impossible.

The result of this pathological fear of our own fragility as human beings is the despair and hopelessness that lie just beneath the surface of our most successful communities and families. To scratch that well-manicured surface is to discover the silent desperation that manifests itself in a myriad of self-destructive ways, from chronic depression, to every conceivable form of addiction, to destroyed and destructive relationships, to suicide—simply the literal expression of the internal suicide we have already committed when we wall ourselves off from others and, therefore, from ourselves. Thus, the suicide rate among suburban white males—the highest for any demographic group—is simply the corollary of the murder rate among inner-city African American and Latino males. The former is a direct result of our failure to confront the latter.

The most threatening others are precisely those who are the weakest, most powerless and fragile, for these represent the repressed, dangerous memory of our common mortality. A direct, intimate relationship thus exists between the struggle for social justice and the possibility of authentic Christian worship, the expression of gratitude for a life that is not ours but is pure gift. The act of solidarity with the wounded other is, at the same time, an acknowledgment of our common woundedness, our common powerlessness. Such solidarity also acknowledges our complicity in the infliction of those wounds. For that reason, we must continue to erect geographical, social, cultural, racial, economic, and psychological barriers between ourselves and them, so that we will not have to face them, and thus face ourselves. In the end, what we fear most is not those persons but ourselves—our weak, fragile, vulnerable, wounded selves. So we avoid touching—or even seeing—the wounds. We avoid risking the act of solidarity, or companionship with the victims of history.[16]

DANGEROUS MEMORIES

Like Christ himself, the crucified victims of history bear the wounds of their suffering and that of past generations; they are Christ's companions on a journey whose goal of resurrection-reconciliation is already experienced in the midst of that com-panionship ("sharing bread with"). The wounds remain visible not in order to condemn but in order to call forth that conversion that alone makes possible an authentic reconciliation, in order to help the doubting Thomases of the first world see themselves mirrored and implicated in those wounds. The resurrected Christ is—and can only be—the crucified Christ.

This Christ is also, therefore, the companion of Latino/a communities in our own histories, where resurrection remains always marked by the memories of suffering, violence, and struggle—what Johann Baptist Metz has called "dangerous memories," for they "make demands on us."[17] They are dangerous, also, precisely because they can never be erased; no amount of future success or liberation can wipe away the wounds, the price paid for that success or liberation. As the German Jewish philosopher Walter Benjamin reminds us, "Every great work of civilization is at the same time a work of barbarism."[18] Every resurrection involves a passion and a death, even if they are only in the form of wounds or scars—that is, dangerous memories.

For the United States, Latinos and Latinas are among those historically marginalized groups that represent "dangerous memories," wounds on the American Dream. To look into the scarred faces and hands of the Salvadoran day laborer standing in a parking lot at dawn, pleading for work to support his family back home, or to place one's hand in the side of the bullet-ridden body of the Puerto Rican boy whose young life has been traded for an even younger pair of Nike sneakers, is to recognize in their bodies the price of resurrection, the cost of success. The bodies of the poor are reminders that, whether or not we stand at the end of history, what is certain is that the history of the victims has not ended:

> What has ended, perhaps, is the history of grand ideological dramas, of divine deceptions, of grand justifications for supposed gestures of progress. ... But the history of the victims does not appear to have ended, the subversive memory that reveals how our presumed greatness was composed simply of blood and death.[19]

The temptation to think of itself as standing at the end of history is particularly strong for the United States. Unique among nations, the United States has no common history that extends beyond the modern period. Indeed, the United States was founded precisely as a rejection of the past, a new city on the hill, a new Jerusalem. As such, the forging of this new nation demanded the eradication of all vestiges of the past, including those peoples who happened to be living on the land that had been chosen for this bold experiment; the nation would be created *ex nihilo* on virgin land, in the wilderness. The price of liberation, the barbaric costs of civilization, would thus be simply wiped away; history would be wiped clean. The American project thus presupposed the possibility of a pure history, a civilization unmarked by barbarism, a resurrection without any remaining signs of the crucifixion. We have destroyed even the ruins of our progress.

The history of Latin America was quite different. The Spanish conquest and colonization did not seek the creation of a new historical reality but the incorporation of this new world into the nascent Spanish empire. For this purpose, the outright extermination of the native populations would be counterproductive; what was required was the assimilation and pacification of the Amerindians. The new lands were not seen primarily as virgin territory for the establishment of new colonies but as repositories of natural resources that could be mined and exported back to Spain to fund the Crown's imperial projects in the wake of the *reconquista*. To this end, the Amerindians would be enslaved, gathered into *encomiendas*, and used as a source of labor.

If nevertheless millions were brutally murdered, and more millions fell victim to the diseases brought by the Europeans, these outcomes were byproducts of the imperial designs of the conquistadores, not an intrinsic aspect of the colonizing ideology, as it was among the English settlers in the North. While the modern drive for territorial expansion and domination was at the heart of both the Iberian and British colonization of the Americas, the processes of expansion developed differently in the North and South:

> The difference was that in the north it was possible and convenient to push back the native inhabitants rather than to conquer and subdue them. What northern colonialists wanted was land [rather than slave labor]. The original inhabitants were a hindrance. So, instead of subjugating the Indians, they set about to push them off their lands, and eventually to exterminate them. If the myth in the Spanish colonies was

that the Indians were like children who needed someone to govern them, the myth in the English colonies was that the Indians were nonpeople; they didn't exist, their lands were a vacuum. In north Georgia, in the middle of Cherokee County, there is a monument to a white man who was, so the monument says, "the first man to settle in these parts." And this, in a county that is still called "Cherokee"! This contrast in the colonizing process led to a "border" mentality in Mexico and much of Latin America, and a "frontier" mentality in the United States.[20]

The violence of conquest in Latin America thus did not exclude the possibility of *mestizaje* (racial-cultural mixture). Even if often through the violent raping of indigenous women, a mixing of indigenous and European races took place that would mark the history of Latin America until today. The wounds of Latin American history could not be erased, for they were inscribed on the mestizo faces of its people, in their language, cultures, and religions. U.S. Hispanics cannot escape their dangerous memories, however hard some may try; the memories make demands of everyone, including the victims. At some profound level, all Hispanics know that Latin America is the child of violence, the European conquistador and the indigenous mother:

> Hispanics . . . always knew that our ancestors were not guiltless. Our Spanish ancestors took the lands of our Indian ancestors. Some of our Indian ancestors practiced human sacrifice and cannibalism. Some of our Spanish forefathers raped our Indian foremothers. Some of our Indian foremothers betrayed their people in favor of the invaders. It is not a pretty story. But it is more real than the story that white settlers came to this land with pure motivations, and that any abuse of its inhabitants was the exception rather than the rule. It is also a story resulting in a painful identity.[21]

Hispanics are, in turn, a dangerous memory for the United States, the cost of U.S. economic and political expansion, however liberating this may have been. Whether through the annexation of half of Mexico in 1848, through the U.S. victory in the Spanish-

American War, or though the so-called stabilization of Central American countries under the U.S. Marines, the United States has laid the groundwork for its economic and political successes—and for the waves of Latin American immigration that so many now perceive as threatening. But an acknowledgment of this fact would necessarily call into question the United States' very identity as the New Jerusalem. "It is precisely in that willful innocence," warns Justo González, "that guilt lies."[22] "The reason why this country has refused to hear the truth in its own history," he continues, "is that as long as it is innocent of such truth, it does not have to deal with the injustices that lie at the heart of its power and its social order."[23] The reason that the wounds must be exposed and the dangerous memories recalled is not to ascribe blame to some while exonerating others. The reason is that only when we are honest about our present and past reality can we more effectively bring our future reality into harmony with our national ideals. (After all, repressed memories live on under the surface and continue to resurface in barbaric ways, such as attacks against immigrants and anyone whose existence recalls those dangerous memories.) To serve as just such a reminder is, according to González,

> one of our functions as a Hispanic minority in this country. It is not a pleasant function, for few love those who destroy the myths by which they live. But it is a necessary function that we must courageously fulfill. . . . In our country, such guilty innocence is the handmaiden of injustice. Injustice thrives on the myth that the present order is somehow the result of pure intentions and a guiltless history. . . . Perhaps once we are agreed that we are all *ladrones* [thieves], it will be easier for all of us to see more clearly into issues of justice.[24]

Perhaps our country will treat its Latinos and Latinas differently when it acknowledges that the Hispanic presence here, in U.S. cities and towns, is a direct result of this country's progress. Can our society admit that that progress, however extraordinary, has nevertheless come at great cost, a cost that our entire nation is currently paying—whether in the physical poverty of our blighted inner cities, the spiritual poverty of our gated suburbs, or our national estrangement from such a large portion of humanity?

JESUS CHRIST: THE WAY, THE TRUTH, AND THE LIFE

Of its very essence, then, the truth of Christ's claims (and the claims of Christians through the ages) is an embodied truth—namely, that of the crucified and risen Lord who continues to accompany us today. The Christian faith is an inherently sacramental faith; it exists only in embodied, incarnate form. The paradigm of that embodiment is the Christ who presented himself to his disciples after the resurrection, wounded yet glorified. Christ invited the disciples to acknowledge a peculiar kind of truth, one that could be known only insofar as they were willing to participate in it—that is, only insofar as they were willing to place their hands in his wounds, acknowledge their complicity in his crucifixion, receive Christ's forgiveness, and then sit down to break bread with him. To know the truth is to become a participant in the life of the crucified and risen Christ, which in turn implies a participation in the lives of those peoples who are themselves crucified victims, those whose wounded bodies are the mirrors of our souls.

The task of the remainder of this book is to explore some of the implications of this assertion. I suggest that, while many of those implications have been either forgotten or ignored in Euro-American Catholicism, they remain visible in U.S. Latino/a Catholic communities. Consequently, the popular religious practices of U.S. Latinos and Latinas are a vital resource for a U.S. Catholic Church struggling to find ways of proclaiming the truth of Christ in our contemporary, twenty-first-century context.

However, as I further suggest, the significance of U.S. Latino/a popular Catholicism cannot be appreciated within a liberal-conservative ideological spectrum. More importantly, the truth of the Christian faith cannot be adequately proclaimed and articulated within such an ideological context; in both its liberal and conservative variants, U.S. Catholicism remains beholden to a fundamentally rationalistic worldview incapable of appreciating the fundamentally participatory character of the Christian truth. The contemporary conflict between liberals and conservatives in the U.S. Catholic Church is a conflict between siblings whose common progenitor is an Enlightenment rationalism suspicious of bodily, lived existence.

I set forth this argument by placing into conversation what I consider three of the most important contemporary resources for articulating a participatory understanding of Jesus Christ as the Way, the Truth, and the Life. These resources are U.S. Latino/a popular Catholicism, Latin American liberation theology, and theological aesthetics. At their best, all three represent dangerous memories of a sacramental faith that makes demands on us: faith in the crucified and risen Christ.

2

Reconciliation in Christ

Christian Truth as the Refusal to Impose Truth

More than forty-five years had passed since I had last peered out an airplane window at the turquoise terminal building. It was exactly as I remembered it. So were the huge white block letters on the façade: "Aeropuerto Internacional Jose Martí—Habana." Back then, I was a six-year-old awaiting a flight to who-knows-where for who-knows-how-long. Through that impenetrable airplane window, I waved anxiously at my father and grandfather, not knowing if or when I would see them again. The scene would remain forever seared in my memory.

By the grace of God, our family eventually reunited in Miami. Now, more than four decades later, I was returning to be reunited with a land and a people that had given me birth. I had no idea how I, who had fled with my family and found success in the United States, would be received by the Cubans on the island. Like an orphan returning to meet his parents after forty-five years, I was deeply anxious. After all, during those four decades, the people of Cuba and the Cuban exile community in the United States had seemingly become estranged. Even as many Cuban Americans had achieved economic and political success in the United States, a large number also harbored tremendous animosity toward Cubans on the island, identifying them with the dictatorial regime under which they lived. How would the impoverished, beaten-down Cuban people who struggled to survive in such desperate circumstances receive me, knowing I had fled with my family? Would they resent me? Would they feel that I, along with the other hundreds of thousands of Cuban exiles, had abandoned them to their plight?

It did not take long for my fears to be assuaged. Wherever I went on the island, the Cuban people's response to my visit was the same: "Thank you for not forgetting us; thank you for remembering us." Whatever survivor's guilt I may have experienced in steeling myself for the trip dissipated in the face of the stunning hospitality of the people. I, who in some very real sense had abandoned them, was now being welcomed back with open arms, no questions asked—not with a "How dare you?" but with a thank-you. Everywhere I went, the message I received was the same: "You are one of us; welcome back."

My experience of being welcomed by those who themselves were victims is, of course, hardly unique. In April 2006, the *Boston Globe* published the story of young Kai Leigh Harriott, a five-year-old African American girl who had been paralyzed when a stray bullet severed her spine as she sat playing on the porch of her house in inner-city Boston. The *Globe* described the scene at the trial of Anthony Warren, the man who had shot Kai Leigh:

> The little girl said the word porch and then began sobbing loudly. After her mother comforted her, 5-year-old Kai Leigh Harriott looked up from her blue wheelchair in the hushed courtroom yesterday and faced the man who fired the stray gunshot that paralyzed her nearly three years ago. "What you done to me was wrong," the dimpled girl with purple and yellow plastic ties in her braids said softly. "But I still forgive him." . . . Yesterday, in emotionally wrenching victim-impact statements that left many spectators in tears, Kai and four members of her family told a Suffolk Superior Court judge that the shooting had changed their lives forever, but had also shown them the value of forgiveness. "We're not victims here; we're victors," said Kai's mother, Tonya David, addressing the court. Moments later, Warren, 29, a convicted felon who pleaded guilty yesterday to avoid a trial, approached Kai and her family and, in barely audible tones, apologized. David recalled his words later. "I'm sorry for what I've done to you and your family," she said Warren told her. "I was known in the street for all the wrong reasons, and now I want to be known for the right reasons." David shook his handcuffed right hand and embraced him.[1]

The following day's newspaper article then reported the following exchange: "Asked by a reporter why she [Kai] forgave the man who shot her, she shyly but clearly said: 'I wanted him to tell the world the truth.' Warren had for three years denied the shooting, but changed his plea Thursday."[2]

Among the victims of our society and world—that is, among the very persons in whom one would expect to find a profound anger and resentment—what one often discovers is an astonishing hospitality, gratitude, and forgiveness. Ironically, it is more often the powerful who harbor anger and resentment against the powerless, rather than the reverse. The successful Cuban American resents the Cuban who stayed behind. The successful suburbanite is enraged at the demands of the urban poor. The successful third-generation immigrant attacks the recent immigrant. The upstanding citizen refuses to forgive the African American man who shot Kai Leigh.

In this chapter, I present an extended reflection on the theological and ethical significance of the victim's (the "saint's"!) offer of forgiveness and reconciliation to his or her oppressor. First I suggest that, when we read the Gospel narratives through the lens of this experience, we discover that the victim's offer of forgiveness and the subsequent reconciliation are at the very heart of the Christian understanding of resurrection; Jesus Christ's resurrection makes possible our reconciliation to God and to each other precisely as the innocent, crucified victim's offer of forgiveness to those who have crucified him. Second, after the resurrection, the basis of reconciliation (strictly speaking) can no longer be justice—not even justice for the victim; forgiveness, or mercy, now becomes the ground of communion with God and each other. Third, the peculiarly Christian approach to social justice includes, as an intrinsic moment in the process of reconciliation, the refusal to impose the truth. Finally, God's reconciling mercy is mediated by the *ecclesia crucis*, the suffering body of Christ in the world, embodied particularly in the crucified people. Needless to say, important qualifications must accompany these ambiguous statements; I suggest these qualifications later. Nevertheless, the necessity for such qualifications should not blind us to the central Christian claim that the person of Jesus Christ presents a radically new form of reconciliation, one whose ground is the crucified and risen Victim, the Lamb of God.

As I argued in the previous chapter, the wounds on Jesus' glorified body can be seen not only as evidence of the bodily resurrection but as the instruments of reconciliation; Jesus' invitation to "put your finger here" makes possible Thomas's response: "My Lord and my God!" Indeed, there is no indication that Thomas ever touched the wound. Jesus' invitation itself provokes conversion. Jesus' invitation to touch and see his wounds is put forth not as a sign of condemnation for Thomas's betrayal and unbelief but as an overture of forgiveness and an invitation to reconciliation: "Peace be with you."

When the crucifixion and resurrection of Jesus Christ are thus interpreted not only as events in the life of the individual Jesus Christ but as events in the life of Jesus Christ as the head of the community he founded, we see that what the resurrection embodies is not simply the victory of individual life over death but the victory of communal life over estrangement, the possibility of reconciliation in the face of abandonment. That reconciliation is made possible by (a) the fact that the physical wounds of betrayal remain visible on the body of the risen Christ, (b) the risen victim's invitation to touch and see his wounds, (c) the character of that invitation as an offer of pardon and an invitation to reconciliation, (d) the apostles' acceptance of Jesus' offer ("They gave him a piece of baked fish" . . . "My Lord and my God"), and finally (e) the radical transformation of the apostles from a group of cowering cowards to a courageous band of disciples willing to literally lay down their lives for their crucified and risen friend and for each other.[3]

A NEW LOGIC

In his passion, death, and resurrection, Jesus Christ thus incarnates, lives out, and makes historical the parable of the Prodigal Son. Jesus here becomes the prodigal father who, though having been abandoned, rushes out to welcome home his wayward son before the son even has a chance to say, "I'm sorry." That story, too, ends with a meal, a celebration. True reconciliation, true community, is made possible only when the demands of justice are transformed by an extravagant, gratuitous love that, still bearing the wounds of betrayal, pardons without counting the cost. The victim thus makes possible the reconciled community—by refusing to impose the truth revealed by the victim's wounds (since to do so, as I've suggested above, would be to deny that very truth).

We can now begin to see the intrinsic relationship between the demands of social solidarity and justice, on the one hand, and the imperative of forgiveness on the other. Indeed, Gustavo Gutiérrez avers that the two principal themes of the Scriptures are the gratuity of God's love and God's preferential love for the poor. Jesus Christ reveals the privileged position of the innocent victim as the mediator of God's extravagant, unexpected mercy. The ability to receive that mercy is thus dependent on our solidarity with the victims. If God's mercy is unanticipated it will be encountered, above all, in those places and among those persons whom our society has deemed ungodly, unlovable. In wholly unexpected ways, they become the bearers of God's mercy. These are the crucified people through whom we encounter the crucified and risen Christ today—not because of who they are, since they are not inherently any more saintly or because they sin less than anyone else, but because of where they are located, on the cross alongside Jesus. Through the innocent victims of history, Jesus thus extends a forgiveness that transforms the logic of justice, the logic of *suum cuique* ("to each what is due him or her"). The economy of human rights is transformed by the aneconomy of the gift, which cannot be demanded but can only be received:

> Jesus' teaching is about how freedom involves not being moved by any over-against, not being creatures of reaction.
> . . . The teaching is about how to relate to the social other as a gift, rather than a burden which defines and limits us. That which makes this movement possible is the forgiving victim, mediated to us in the transformation of human relationality.[4]

In our contemporary world, the economy of human rights necessarily remains trapped within the logic of an acquisitive, consumerist capitalism. Reconciliation is thus conceived as the proper distribution of rights, which are themselves viewed as commodities to be acquired and redistributed. Even when the proper balance of rights is achieved, the underlying antagonism and competition remain, the agonistic logic of conflict still grounds the communal relationships. Only the victim's act of forgiveness can rupture that logic: "Capitalism does not know, short of repressing it, what to do with forgiveness."[5] So, for example,

> At the end of the 1970s in Latin America, when the weight of the growing external debt was beginning to be felt, the liturgy of both Catholic and Protestant Churches across the continent underwent a subtle alteration. The language of the Our Father was altered from "Forgive us our debts" to "Forgive us our offenses." This change . . . was instigated by economic pressures. Capitalists feared that persons would begin to see that Christian forgiveness presented a direct challenge to the current economic order. They could not abide the Churches forming persons who, by receiving and extending the gift of forgiveness, would defy the justice of capitalism's markets.[6]

Moreover, not only is the logic of *suum cuique* unable to resist the logic of capitalist consumption, that logic will necessarily fail by its own criteria since, ultimately, one can never undo past injustice; the wounds forever remain on the body of the risen Christ. The history of suffering remains forever an intrinsic part of the history of progress. The crowing cock and the pieces of silver remain forever inscribed in the history of the resurrection. The Trail of Tears and Jim Crow remain forever inscribed in the history of American progress. Thus, only the gift of forgiveness offers the possibility of a genuine novelty and hope:

> By abandoning calculi of reciprocity and desert, forgiveness sets both the victim and the victimizer free from the unbearable burden of injustice. The victim is freed from the enmity that is born of a violation that cannot be undone; the victimizer is freed from the guilt and loathing that comes from never being able to undo the violation. Forgiveness places them both in a position to risk a new relationship. Ultimately forgiveness is an act of hope that denies the destructiveness

of injustice the final word, instead insisting that something else is always possible.[7]

Despite the ethical arguments for forgiveness, however, ultimately the warrant for the logic of gift over the logic of justice is explicitly and specifically theological: the logic of gift "more accurately reflects the character of God" as revealed in the crucified and risen Christ, and thus more accurately reflects the call to Christian discipleship.[8]

WHITHER JUSTICE?

Despite my argument thus far, I am well aware that justice is also at the heart of the Christian call to discipleship and reflects the character of God as this is revealed in Scripture, from the Prophets to the twenty-fifth chapter of Matthew's Gospel. I am also aware that the logic of forgiveness is susceptible to all sorts of dangerous distortions that, in the past as today, have promoted passivity in the face of oppression and, indeed, undermined the process of reconciliation. One need not go very far to find examples of victims being exhorted to "forgive and forget," whether Jews who are encouraged to get over the Holocaust, African Americans urged to let the bygones of slavery be bygones, or victims of abuse encouraged to get on with their lives.

The call to reconciliation in no way obviates the struggle for social justice in defense of the intrinsic dignity of the person and the rights that would safeguard that dignity. Rather, as Gustavo Gutiérrez insists, we must "situate justice within the framework of God's gratuitous love."[9] A praxis of solidarity with the poor in their struggle for justice is the means by which we receive God's mercy and the gift of forgiveness. "Forgiveness may be gratuitous," notes Christian Duquoc, "but it is not arbitrary; it calls for a change of attitude on the part of the offender or sinner, who enters into a new relationship with the person who forgives. This goes by the name of conversion."[10] This new relationship is one of solidarity in the struggle for justice, in what José González Faus has called "the revolution of a forgiven people."[11] The victim and former oppressor now join the struggle not out of a sense of either duty or rights, which still imply an underlying conflict, but out of a shared gratitude for the unanticipated grace that made reconciliation possible. In their shared gratitude for the gift of reconciliation, both oppressor and victim are liberated. "The *forgiveness of acceptance* bestowed by Jesus in the gospel accounts," observes Jon Sobrino, "is something *not merely beneficial, but liberating.*"[12] Both are liberated from themselves, argues Sobrino; "it is the gratitude of knowing oneself to be accepted," he suggests, "that moves a person to a de-centering from self."[13]

The gratuitous mercy of God compels a praxis of solidarity. The act of forgiveness generates repentance, conversion, and solidarity in the struggle for justice; Thomas's "My Lord and my God" is preceded by Jesus' "Peace be with you." It is not repentance that brings about forgiveness, but the reverse. Sobrino explains that, in the person of Jesus Christ, forgiveness is always the starting point for any consideration of sin:

> The divine mystagogia into a recognition of sin in all its seriousness operates from a point of departure in forgiveness. Nor let it be thought that this is somehow an easier, softer way. Human beings may well prefer to cling to that which is of themselves, be it their sin, rather than be delivered from it, if the price to be paid is to be forgiven gratuitously. . . . It is the acceptance that is forgiveness that adequately and wholly discloses the fact that I am a sinner and gives me the strength to acknowledge myself as such and change radically. The conversion demanded so radically by Jesus is preceded by the offer of God's love. It is not conversion that requires God to accept the sinner; rather, just contrariwise, it is God's acceptance that makes conversion possible.[14]

The apostles remained paralyzed by fear until the crucified and risen Christ confronted them with his wounds, demanding that they acknowledge the wounds, yet offering pardon and reconciliation. Only then could Thomas confess, "My Lord and my God." The convicted criminal Anthony Warren remained paralyzed by his fear of the law until his victim, the five-year-old Kai Leigh Harriott, confronted him with her wounds: "What you done to me was wrong, but I still forgive you." Only then could Warren admit, "I'm sorry for what I've done to you and your family," and declare that "I was known in the street for all the wrong reasons, and now I want to be known for the right reasons." Forgiveness compels confession and repentance, and repentance implies a commitment to justice: "Now I want to be known for the right reasons." Genuine forgiveness is based on truth, on an "honesty about the real" (in Sobrino's words). The offer and reception of God's gratuitous mercy thus implies judgment and confession, not as extrinsic but as integral to the act of reconciliation itself.[15]

Sobrino goes so far as to say that solidarity with the victim "constitutes a kind of reparation . . . for what was done in the past."[16] Ultimately, full reparation for past suffering is impossible; we can never undo past injustices, and those injustices will always remain part of our present and future. What we *can* do is to reconstitute our relationships on a completely different foundation based on mercy, confession, penance, and solidarity. Restoration can then be understood, not as a making up for what was done in the past, but as the process of reconciliation itself. This step indeed involves restitution, giving back or redistributing resources, but the goal of such redistribution is not establishing a status quo ante—which is impossible, in any case—but the reconciliation of oppressor and oppressed, the constitution of a reconciled community; the focus is not on the what of restitution but on the who. Justice is ultimately not a question of protecting rights but of nurturing communion.[17]

Characterized by this process of forgiveness, confession, penance, and solidarity, the struggle for justice is thus the mode in which we receive mercy. Since reconciliation implies not only an offer but an acceptance of forgiveness, without justice there can be no true reconciliation or, for that matter, no true forgiveness: "Forgiveness entails repentance. . . . Repentance, therefore, is not a condition of forgiveness but rather the means of its reception."[18] The new or renewed commitment to justice is the expression of repentance and the means of a true reconciliation based on forgiveness.

The commitment to justice that is intrinsic to reconciliation, then, precludes any interpretation of reconciliation that would demand or even expect that the victim make an offer of forgiveness, thereby blaming the victim for the failure of reconciliation. Without justice there can be neither reconciliation nor forgiveness, because both imply the oppressor's reception of the offer in the form of repentance and a commitment to justice.

THE REFUSAL TO IMPOSE THE TRUTH OF CHRIST

The crucified and risen Christ offers a forgiveness that overturns the logic of *suum cuique*. So wherever innocent victims, the crucified people, extend an offer of forgiveness, that offer implies a refusal to coerce justice or impose the truth; by refusing to impose the truth even on the oppressor, the victim makes true reconciliation and liberation possible, a new way of relating based not on conflict and competition but on mercy. The victims' offer of mercy implies the refusal to impose the truth on others—including the oppressor—through an act of coercion precisely because the truth of the crucified and risen Christ cannot be imposed without inherent contradiction. The offer of mercy assures that the victim's suffering remains visible for all to see, that any future reconciliation or justice includes the wounds as dangerous memories rather than pretend that, once justice is achieved and all wrongs have been righted, the wounds have been forever healed. The apostles would have much preferred to have the risen Christ appear to them without his wounds, but then true reconciliation would not have been possible. True reconciliation presupposes a forgiveness that includes the wounds: "What you done to me was wrong, but I still forgive you. . . . Put your finger here. . . ."

This is not to glorify suffering itself, which is always an evil. Indeed, true forgiveness implies an acknowledgment that the wounds are real and unjust, that the victim is indeed innocent: "What you done to me was wrong. . . ." The refusal to deny the suffering is thus not an end in itself. Rather, that refusal is the necessary corollary of the victim's offer of forgiveness, the corollary of God's gratuitous grace as embodied in the crucified and risen Savior. "The ultimate basis of God's preference for the poor," argues Gutiérrez, "is to be found in God's own goodness and not in any analysis of society or in human compassion, however pertinent these reasons may be."[19] The ultimate basis for the struggle for justice is to be found in God, not in us; it is precisely this belief that is affirmed in the victim's act of forgiveness. "Christian forgiveness," argues Daniel Bell, "is not simply one of a handful of social strategies the Church has at its disposal for the sake of reducing conflict; it is primarily a witness to God and what God in Christ is doing in the world to overcome sin. . . . The refusal to cease suffering that is forgiveness is ultimately an act of hope in God."[20] Gutiérrez refers to the crucified and risen Christ as God's "wager": "In sending his Son, the Father 'wagered' on the possibility of a faith and behavior characterized by gratuitousness and by a response to the demand that justice be established. When history's 'losers' . . . follow in the steps of Jesus, they are seeing to it that the Lord wins his wager."[21] The crucified people, argues Bell, make their own wager, a wager on God: "They are wagering that God is who the Gospel proclaims God to be, the one who defeats sin and wipes away every tear, not with the sword of a justice that upholds rights but with the gift of forgiveness in Christ."[22]

Consequently, the refusal to impose truth is not a passive acquiescence in suffering that eschews the struggle for justice. The refusal to impose truth is simply the acknowledgment that the struggle for justice is not an end in itself but mediates God's mercy in the world; the struggle for justice is the privileged place where we encounter and respond to a grace that overcomes the logic of *suum cuique*. As Gutiérrez explains,

> We in Latin America are also convinced . . . that in the liberation process we are capable of creating our own idols for ourselves. For example, the idol of justice: it might seem strange to say this but justice can become an idol if it is not placed in the context of gratuity. . . . Gratuity is the framework for justice and gives it meaning in history. Social justice, no matter how important it is—and it is—can also be an idol, and we have to purify ourselves of this to affirm very clearly that only God suffices and to give justice itself the fullness of its meaning.[23]

The refusal to impose truth is our way of participating in God's own gratuitous praxis in history, a praxis in which reconciliation is mediated by the wounds of crucifixion—but only when those wounds are acknowledged as real ("Put your finger here") and when the offer of mercy is received through repentance and conversion ("My Lord and my God"). Indeed, as noted above, where there is no repentance and conversion, there is no true mercy, because the act of forgiveness implies both offer and reception. (If I am convinced that I am not a sinner, that I am in no need of forgiveness. I cannot be forgiven, no matter how much God, or my victim, may desire to forgive me; this is, by definition, the only unforgivable sin.) The offer of mercy in the face of injustice is itself a witness against the evil that is suffering. However, if it is perceived as such, such witness compels action. As Sobrino argues, reconciliation demands more than simply recognizing the wounds, more than simply asking "what have I done to crucify" wounded victims; it also demands that I ask, "What am I doing to take them down from the cross? What ought I to do that a crucified people may rise again?"[24]

THE CRUCIFIED PEOPLE AND THE *ECCLESIA CRUCIS*: A PRIVILEGED MODE OF BEING CHURCH

The preferential option for the poor is nothing other than the assertion that the crucified people of history are the privileged mediators of God's mercy in the church and the world.[25] The crucified people are the privileged historical mediation of the crucified and risen Christ in the world. When they extend mercy, they embody Christ's own offer to the apostles after the resurrection: "Peace be with you." It is a mercy that judges and demands justice even as it makes reconciliation possible; indeed, it makes reconciliation possible precisely because it judges. Yet, in doing so, the crucified people embody the good news that "there is another way to live."[26]

As mediators of the crucified and risen Christ not only in the world but also in the Church, the crucified people also remind us that suffering is one of the marks of the church. Indeed, it may be time to emphasize again the biblical notion of the *ecclesia crucis* (so central for Paul and Luther):

No other single ecclesiological theme receives the attention that the suffering of the church receives in our textual sources. For centuries theology has maintained that the true marks of the church are the four that are named in the Nicene Creed: "one, holy, catholic, and apostolic church." . . . Each of these *notae ecclesia* can find some biblical basis, but none of them can claim a fraction of the attention paid to the theme of the church's suffering in these sacred writings. . . . The earliest and most prominent manner of discerning the true church and distinguishing it from false claims to Christian identity was to observe the nature and extent of the suffering experienced by a community of faith. Why? Because, of course, as Paul makes clear . . . if you claim to be a disciple of the crucified one you must expect to participate in his sufferings; . . . you will have to become a *community* of the cross.[27]

To the extent, therefore, that the crucified people reveal the church as a crucified church, they mediate Christ's own mercy in the world and in the church. "Now this has consequences!" observes British Catholic theologian James Alison. "It means that holiness is our dependence on the forgiveness of the victim. That is to say, our being holy is dependent on the resurrection of the forgiving victim."[28] (And we ourselves are responsible for helping make that resurrection possible, for "taking the crucified people down from the cross"!) The preferential option for the poor, for the victims, is thus always a preferential option for all, since we are all dependent on the victims' mercy if we are to live freely in a reconciled community where there is no need for victims; Christ himself offered this to his disciples as he appeared to them after his resurrection:

What is given in Christ's victim death is a subversion of the old human way of belonging, and the possibility of our induction into a new human way of belonging, of being-with, without any over-against. This means that justification by faith belongs, in the first place, to the new community, the group receiving as a given its unity from the forgiving victim. It is exactly this making present of the beginnings of a new reconciled humanity which is the making present of justification by faith in the world.[29]

This indeed is what the risen Jesus offers his estranged apostles when he greets them: "Peace be with you." The *ecclesia* is thus at its heart an *ecclesia crucis* precisely insofar as it is the community constituted by the forgiving victim who demands an acknowledgment of the unjust wounds ("Put your fingers here") even as he extends mercy to his oppressor.

"The Spirit of Jesus is in the poor," asserts Jon Sobrino, "and, with them as his point of departure, he re-creates the entire Church. If this truth is understood in all its depth and in an authentically Trinitarian perspective, it means that the history of God advances indefectibly by way of the poor; that the Spirit of Jesus takes historical flesh in the poor; and that the poor show the direction of history that is in accord with God's plan."[30] In no way does this suggest a "parallel church"; rather it specifies the privileged (not exclusive) sociohistorical locus wherein the church *is* church and discovers what it means to *be* church. Neither does this understanding obviate the need for an official magisterium; rather, it proposes (again, based on the gospel) the way in which the magisterial authority ought to function—namely, in solidarity with history's victims. The ecclesiological image of the church of the crucified people posits not a new church but "a new mode of being the Church."[31]

Inspired by Archbishop Oscar Romero and Ignacio Ellacuría, friends who had shared the common fate of those who identify with the poor, Sobrino holds that if "the Spirit of Jesus takes historical flesh in the poor," if the poor are the privileged mediators of that Spirit not only in the world, but within the Church herself (not because they are necessarily morally superior but simply because they are poor), then the very historicity and corporeality of the poor is itself the privileged locus for encountering Jesus' flesh, the body of Christ in the world today. The categories of "the poor" or "the victims" take on an explicitly theological character as the crucified people, *el pueblo crucificado*. The crucified people are the privileged historical mediation of the crucified and risen Christ in the world. As mediators of the crucified and risen Christ not only in the world, but also in the church, the crucified people also remind us that suffering is one of the marks of the church.

To say that suffering is a mark of the church is to privilege the crucified people and to demand solidarity with the victims as the privileged praxis through which we demonstrate ourselves to be church. "Hence," as Shawn Copeland notes, "the community of believers, the *ekklesia*, the church ought to be recognizable in its willingness to stand beside the poor, injured, despised, and excluded sufferers in history, in its willingness to suffer."[32] "Like Jesus," she continues, "the church must be willing to risk fortune and future for the sake of those who are abandoned to the scrap heap of history. Above all, these children, women, and men must be loved, for in their suffering they bear the mark of the crucified Jesus, who is no one else than the Resurrected Lord."[33]

Here we have, then, the seeds of a rereading of the ecclesiological image "body of Christ." Since the late Middle Ages, the notion of body of Christ as applied to the community of the faithful has become increasingly spiritualized, if not mystified. As Henri de Lubac and other scholars have observed, the term "*corpus mysticum*," or "mystical body of Christ," was not widely used in reference to the church until the late twelfth and early thirteenth centuries. The term "mystical body of Christ" originally appeared in the fifth century and referred not to the church but to the Eucharist; the church was the "*verum corpus*" (true, or real body). The eucharistic controversies of the eleventh century made it necessary to apply this latter term to the Eucharist.[34] If, as Joseph Cardinal Ratzinger posited, the term "*mysticum*" was never intended to mean "mystical" but rather "referring to the Mystery (of the Eucharist)," it does not stretch the imagination to see how "*corpus mysticum*" could have led to a spiritualization of the term "body" as applied to the church, even as the same term, as applied to the Eucharist, became increasingly literalized.[35] De Lubac argued that one result of this shift was an increasing identification of the eucharistic species with the historical body of Christ on the cross. The corollary, it would seem, was an increased gap between the historical body of Christ on the cross and the church. Referring to the Pauline notion of the body of Christ, Gutiérrez observes, "Readers often regard this theology of the church as simply a beautiful metaphor. However, we must, shocking though this idea may be, see through to the realism that characterizes the Pauline approach. He is speaking of the real body of Christ, which he looks upon as an extension of the incarnation."[36]

What Sobrino and Ellacuría are doing, therefore, is retrieving the original connection between the people of God and the historical body of Christ on the cross, while concretizing and specifying that intrinsic connection; what unites the two is the cross or, more precisely, the crucified body. In an analysis of Ellacuría's ecclesiology, Kevin Burke writes as follows:

> As Jesus' Body becomes the sacramental symbol of the salvation he mediates, so too the church's bodiliness enables it to continue making that salvation present in history. As Christology needs to approach the whole mystery of Jesus Christ by beginning from his historical corporeality, ecclesiology needs to approach the salvific sacramentality of the church from its historical corporeality. . . . For the church to be the Body of Christ in history, it must be present to history through particular historical actions that continue and correspond to the life of Jesus. . . . It means the church cannot fulfill its vocation with its back turned to the crucified peoples of our world. On the contrary, it must seek them out, live in solidarity with them, announce God's Good News to them, and reflect to them the truth that they are God's beloved ones.[37]

The *ecclesia crucis* identifies itself with the crucified people, seeks their liberation, and in so doing shares in their suffering. The real body of Christ is thus mediated by the real bodies of the poor, the victims, the marginalized in history.[38]

Both outside and within the church, the crucified people are the privileged locus for encountering today the crucified and risen Lord. In so mediating the wounded and resurrected body of Christ in the world, the church herself is called to a cruciform existence in history. This is true not because the cross is the goal of Christian discipleship, but precisely because it isn't—precisely because Christian discipleship is ultimately not about death but about life. The church thus demonstrates most fully its commitment to life to the extent that it "takes the crucified people down from the cross" (the phrase is that of Sobrino and Ellacuría). Such solidarity leads to and is rooted in the cross not as an end in itself but as the inevitable consequence of the church's mission as sacrament of the reign of God:

> Consequently, the church fulfills its sacramental vocation to mediate salvation to history when it makes concrete both the

critical and constructive demands of the reign of God in each historical situation. The church fulfills the critical demand of God's reign when it prophetically denounces the crucifying powers of the world. It takes up its constructive task when—in deed even more than word—it announces that the reign of God draws near as salvation/liberation of the poor in relation to their terrible situation of captivity and death.[39]

The church becomes a crucified church insofar as it embodies, makes present, and proclaims the reign of God as the continuation in history of Christ's own enactment of that reign. Just as the risen Christ still bears the wounds of crucifixion, so too must the reign of God bear the wounds resulting from its proclamation and enactment in history. The crucified people of God make it possible for us—in Sobrino's words—to be "honest about the real," honest about the real body of Christ, risen yet wounded. Such honesty is not an end in itself but the precondition for proclaiming the possibility of reconciliation, the hope of resurrection.

Christ's resurrection necessarily implies the reconstitution of his community, the gathering together of those disciples who had earlier abandoned him in order, now, to found a community based on forgiveness. Therefore, salvation itself is necessarily relational and communal; there can be no salvation except in and through renewed relationships:

> We find it difficult to understand that justification by grace through faith is necessarily a collective phenomenon. It is collective because the only sort of salvation we have been given is the beginnings of the unity of the whole of humanity in a new society founded on the forgiveness of the risen victim. Grace is automatically collective: there is no grace that does not tend towards the construction of this new Israel of God. There is no faith in Jesus that is not intrinsically related to his founding and edifying this new humanity, and there is no making righteous that does not involve a movement away from a certain sort of social "belonging," kept safe by casting out victims, and a simultaneous movement towards the fraternal construction of the people of the victim present in all the world. . . .[40]

This is not to suggest, however, that the crucified people are themselves identical with the crucified and risen Christ. As Gutiérrez warns, the poor themselves are called to make a preferential option for the poor; the poor themselves can be accomplices in victimization. Likewise, James Alison warns against a simplistic notion of victimhood that merely perpetuates an us-against-them mentality:

> Now, again, the knowledge of Jesus, the crucified and risen victim makes a difference here. For if you know the crucified and risen victim, you know that you are not yourself the victim. The danger is much more that you are either actively, or by omission, or both, a victimizer. We have only one self-giving victim, whose self-giving was quite outside any contamination of human violence or exploitation. The rest of us are all involved with that violence. The person who thinks of himself or herself as the victim is quick to divide the world into "we" and "they." In the knowledge of the risen victim there is only a "we," because we no longer need to define ourselves over against anyone at all.[41]

Insofar as we succumb to the temptation to romanticize the victim, whether ourselves or others, we thus perpetuate the logic of *suum cuique*, which is fundamentally divisive and conflictive rather than unitive.

It is not because of any moral superiority but because of their social location, then, that the crucified people are the privileged locus for encountering today the extravagant, unexpected mercy of the wounded and resurrected Lord. In so mediating that mercy, the victims remind us that all resurrections participate in and are made possible by Christ's own wounded resurrection:

> For what we preach is not ourselves, but Jesus Christ as Lord. . . . But we have this treasure in earthen vessels, to show that the transcendent power belongs to God, and not to us. We are afflicted in every way but not crushed; perplexed, but not driven to despair; persecuted, but not forsaken; struck down, but not destroyed; always carrying in the body the death of Jesus, so that the life of Jesus may also be manifested

in our bodies. For while we live we are always being given up to death for Jesus' sake, so that the life of Jesus may be manifested in our mortal flesh. (2 Cor. 4:5-11)

The crucified people of our world make their preemptive offer of forgiveness "so that the life of Jesus," the crucified and risen Jesus, may be manifested in our oh-so-broken world. By taking the victims down from the cross, we become capable of receiving their offer of mercy and Christ's own offer of life.

3

Popular Catholicism

From "Truth" to Truth

In July 1996, Abbot Guillermo Schulemburg of the Basilica of Our Lady of Guadalupe in Mexico City resigned from his post. A few days earlier, the Mexican media had quoted him as suggesting that Juan Diego, the indigenous man to whom *La Morenita* had appeared on December 9, 1531, was "not a reality." The national uprising that ensued had forced the abbot's resignation. On this side of the border, the reaction was generally one of either incomprehension or bemusement—whether on the part of liberal or conservative Catholics. Yet I don't think we can properly understand the Mexican people's visceral reaction without appreciating the fact that, when they insisted that Juan Diego was indeed real, they were operating with a very different notion of reality than either Schulemburg or Euro-American Catholics, even if these latter sympathized with the plight of the Mexican poor standing up to the overbearing hierarch. Indeed, precisely because contemporary Euro-Americans, including Catholics, are decidedly uncomfortable with any commitment to a particular reality or truth, I suggest, Latino/a Catholics remain misunderstood and depreciated members of the U.S. Catholic community. It is also a principal reason that the reality or truth of the crucified and risen Christ remains itself marginalized alongside the marginalized communities that he continues to accompany even today.

My own experience working in the U.S. Hispanic Catholic community has led me to ask whether most contemporary Euro-American theologies can, in the end, yield an adequate appreciation of U.S. Hispanic popular Catholicism and, more importantly, of the *Cristo Compañero* at the heart of that lived faith, the Christ who is encountered as the most profound reality at the heart of everyday existence, the Christ whose extravagant love for us makes hope possible. In the following pages, I focus on the modern (and, by derivation, postmodern) separation of form and content, or symbol and referent, as impeding such an appreciation and, therefore, impeding our ability to make a preferential option for the poor, our ability to walk in solidarity with the poor and, more specifically, with the God of the poor. When accepted as an a priori criterion for interpreting the lived faith of the poor, the contemporary distrust of so-called commonsense knowledge, or the suspicion of all appearances, leads to a distorted interpretation of that faith. In order to appreciate the theological wisdom of the poor, we must be willing to question the contemporary need to deconstruct all appearances, all that appears as real; the drive to deconstruct must itself be subjected to deconstruction.

Whatever our explicit intentions, the presumptive separation of appearance and reality, or concrete symbol and referent, ultimately results in a privileging of the immaterial and abstract explanation (whether theological, doctrinal, psychological, or sociological) over the material and concrete, and a privileging of theoretical analysis over commonsense knowledge without acknowledging the necessary, intrinsic connections between the poles in each case. In turn, such an epistemological separation distorts our understanding of the nature of reality and the character of human action. Finally, I submit, this distortion obscures the normative character of the crucified and risen Jesus Christ encountered by the poor, especially by Latin Americans and U.S. Latinos and Latinas.

In light of the above, one might be tempted to interpret U.S. Hispanic popular Catholicism in either of two ways: (1) as the expression of an immature, superstitious faith (the modern interpretation), or (2) as a cultural expression of a people that helps provide meaning for their lives and, as such, ought to be respected and affirmed (the postmodern interpretation). Neither of these interpretations allows for the possibility that the lived faith of Latinos and Latinas may actually be true, may accurately reflect reality, and, as such, may make normative claims on non-Hispanics. The modern interpretation simply dismisses the popular faith as a superstition that must be outgrown, while the postmodern interpretation affirms it as meaningful, real, and true, but only for Latinos and Latinas.

Instead, a genuine appreciation of U.S. Hispanic popular Catholicism calls for a critical realism that, without prescinding from critical, scientific analyses of popular religious practices, affirms the credibility of the worldview reflected in these practices. If one cannot accept naively, as literally true and real, the worldview expressed in devotion to Our Lady of Guadalupe, neither can one simply assume a priori that the historicity of Guadalupe is irrelevant . . . unless, that is, one is willing to disregard the experience of the poor and their own interpretation of that experience. My argument, in other words, is that the worldview expressed in Latino/a popular Catholicism is characterized by a critical realism that is not naive or simplistic in its affirmation of religious truth, or in its understanding of reality. On the other hand, neither is popular Catholicism reducible to a mere human construction that, while meaningful for Hispanics, cannot be said to express a truth or reality that extends beyond the U.S. Hispanic community. In short, the faith of the poor as lived and understood by the poor themselves presupposes a truth that transcends the human person and, as such, is revealed to and received by us. While that faith is hardly immune to criticism—nor should it be—such criticism, whether by ecclesiastical officials, theologians, or social scientists, ought to be grounded not only in a practical solidarity with the poor but in a solidarity with the God of the poor, the God who the poor themselves claim is the central reality of their everyday lives. Can we truly be in solidarity with the poor while simultaneously depreciating or even rejecting their most basic assumptions about their own lives? Those assumptions are neither immature nor are they unique to the religious faith of the poor, for they are at the heart of Christian faith: the crucified and risen Christ is really present with us today as the full expression of God's extravagant love for each one of us, a love that alone makes hope and life itself possible, a love that survives death and that empowers us in our everyday struggle against the forces of violence and death in our societies, neighborhoods, families, and churches. Thus, what we call truth is neither purely subjective nor purely objective, but is the performative, participative reality disclosed in the human act of reception-response to this extravagant love with which we have been gifted.

Reality or truth may thus be conceived, analogously, as the image that emerges when a film is projected onto a blank screen; the real involves both an objective dimension (the blank screen) and a subjective dimension (the projector). Simply because a projector is necessary in order to show a film does not mean that the image that appears on the screen is therefore nothing but a projection; without the screen, there would be no image. Simply because the figure of Juan Diego is an expression of the people's hope for liberation does not mean that there was no Juan Diego. Indeed, something—or someone—might have awakened that hope. Simply because Jesus Christ is the answer to the deepest human longing to be fully accepted and loved does not mean that Christ is a figment of our imagination. Indeed, it may be Christ himself who has awakened that longing in us, so that we might seek our fulfillment in him. And this, I suggest, is precisely what the lived faith of the poor presupposes: namely, that God is the ultimate source rather than the product of their—and our—deepest yearning for liberation. Thus, the symbols of God's activity in the world (e.g., Juan Diego) are indeed real, for they are not mere products or even expressions of our hope but, more specifically, the very source of that hope. If we are to understand popular Catholicism, therefore, we must open ourselves to a notion of religious symbol that is much more realistic than our contemporary Western notions of the symbol.

To understand the difference between these notions of religious symbolism, we might examine the different ways of understanding the relationship between a symbol and that which it symbolizes (i.e., the symbol's referent), particularly as the understanding of that relationship has evolved historically. That evolution has resulted in a contemporary understanding of symbol that presupposes a separation between the symbol and its referent (what the symbol symbolizes). Hence, for example, we assume a dichotomy between reality and mere symbols; Juan Diego is merely a symbol, we can claim, and therefore not a reality. Such a notion of symbol can only yield a distorted view of popular Catholicism, whether in the form of an outright rejection of the latter's validity or in the form of a romanticized view of the lived faith of the poor.

The symbolic realism of Latino/a popular Catholicism has historical roots that themselves are linked to the evolving notion of symbol in Western theology; at the heart of popular Catholicism is an understanding of symbol fundamentally at odds with modern Western notions of symbol. Indeed, the liberating character of popular Catholicism is rooted precisely in its premodern (or at least nonmodern) notion of symbol. The liberating character of that premodern notion of symbol stems from the holistic, organic worldview that such a notion of symbol presupposes. If Latino and Latina Catholics have resisted the separation of symbol and referent that characterizes modern and postmodern worldviews, the reason is that U.S. Hispanic popular Catholicism has not (yet, at least) shed its premodern, medieval and baroque roots. If popular Catholicism represents a *ressourcement* (retrieval and renewal) from the margins, these roots are, therefore, among the important sources that Latina and Latino Catholics can help retrieve for the Catholic Church in the United States.

Catholic *ressourcement* thus demands a retrieval of those popular religious traditions that, while perhaps not always recognized in the official theological and liturgical texts or teachings of the Church, are nevertheless an integral part of the *sensus fidei*, the lived faith as a central locus of revelation:

> The *sensus fidei* is an entire spirituality and systematized understanding. It is not merely an attitude of belief. The people of God grasps the entirety of the faith through some axes: the passion of Jesus, an ethic of solidarity, the celebration of life, a communitarian faith, confidence in God, the rejection of evil. . . . How much does this influence professional and academic reflection? It is a pity, because the *sensus fidei* opens the door to truth.[1]

Paraphrasing the famous dictum of Gustavo Gutiérrez, this *sapientia populorum*, the theological wisdom of the poor, represents a challenge not so much to the content of theology but to the way in which we do theology. In the words of Diego Irarrazaval, "The challenge is not to broaden what we are already doing, but to think in a different way. That is, to work methodologically with materials produced by the people and to dialogue critically with the communities that produce them. . . . I refer to five types of materials that constitute 'theological *loci*': icons, scripture reading, narrative theology, testimony, ritual logic."[2]

If Catholicism has something to offer a world seeking a reason for hope, if it has something to offer young persons seeking a way to resist the seductive power of a stupefying consumerist culture, U.S. Latino/a popular Catholicism offers the possibility of retrieving aspects of the Catholic tradition that have been marginalized in (relatively) recent generations but that represent crucial resources for countercultural resistance and social justice. In his Apostolic Exhortation *Ecclesia in America*, Pope John Paul II drew special attention to popular religion as a resource for the church of America (South, Central, and North):

> A distinctive feature of America is an intense popular piety, deeply rooted in the various nations. It is found at all levels and in all sectors of society, and it has special importance as a place of encounter with Christ for all those who in poverty of spirit and humility of heart are sincerely searching for God (cf. *Mt* 11:25). This piety takes many forms: "Pilgrimages to shrines of Christ, of the Blessed Virgin and the Saints, prayer for the souls in purgatory, the use of sacramentals (water, oil, candles . . .). These and other forms of popular piety are an opportunity for the faithful to encounter the living Christ."[3]

If we avoid the modern temptation to understand tradition exclusively in terms of texts, laws, concepts, or confession (all susceptible to rationalist interpretations) and include within our understanding of tradition the lived traditions of the poor, we can avoid both a fundamentalism that identifies tradition with only the relatively recent, modern, rationalist understanding of tradition that characterized Trent and Vatican I, and we can avoid a liberalism that assumes the same rationalist understanding of tradition, though in order to reject or deconstruct tradition.

POPULAR CATHOLICISM AND OFFICIAL
RELIGIOUS PRACTICES

To respond effectively to this increasing Latino/a presence in the church, we must appreciate the significance and richness of U.S. Latino/a popular Catholicism, the Latino/a community's way of being Catholic. In and through their rituals, prayers, processions, devotions, and celebrations, Latinas and Latinos live their Catholic faith. Such popular expressions of faith have ancient roots in Christian tradition; liturgical theologian Keith Pecklers notes that "popular religiosity traces its foundations to the origins of Christianity, and includes devotions, prayers, and pious practices performed by the people, and without the required assistance of clergy, though clergy may be present."[4]

Whether in the *Posadas*, the Christmastime reenactment of Joseph and Mary's search for lodging; or the *mañanitas* sung to Our Lady of Guadalupe on the morning of her feast day; or the *Via Crucis* of Good Friday; or the annual pilgrimage to the holy chapel at Chimayo, New Mexico; or the celebrations on the Day of the Dead; or the family prayers offered on the home altar, Latinas and Latinos experience the palpable, loving presence of a God who walks with us in the daily rhythm of life in family, neighborhood, and community. Consequently, the *manera de ser* (way of being) that I am here calling "popular Catholicism" is, above all, a way of living centered on relationship and, even more specifically, on family—though by family, I do not mean the nuclear family but that extended family that, if extended far enough, ultimately unites us to the larger human—indeed, cosmic—community. The Catholicism of Latinos and Latinas, therefore, tends to be a Catholicism rooted, first, not in the parish but in the home, in the neighborhood.

This fact exacerbates the invisibility of Latino/a Catholics in the U.S. church. Euro-American Catholics are accustomed to gauging church participation, or church size, by looking out into the pews on Sunday mornings or by checking the latest parish registry; the locus of Catholic identity is the parish. For Latino/a Catholics, on the other hand, the locus of identity is not so much the parish as the home.

The reasons for this situation are many, including some important historical reasons. For centuries, Latino/a Catholics—particularly those who live in rural areas—have not had access to clergy. Throughout Latin America, millions of Catholics have no access to a priest except once every month or two when a circuit-rider comes into town to celebrate Mass, hear confessions, perform baptisms, and so on. Moreover, that priest is not likely to be native-born; even today, the vast majority of Catholic priests in Latin America are foreign-born—and this in a continent that contains half of all the world's Catholics. So, if the home is the center of worship for Latin American and Latino/a Catholics, this is to a great extent out of necessity; if the faith was going to be nurtured, it would have to be nurtured by the people themselves. Popular Catholicism, then, is truly popular—that is, truly "of the people"—in that its roots are not clerical but fundamentally lay. The ministers who look after the day-to-day spiritual well-being of the community are not the priests but the *abuelitas*.

The problem is exacerbated when Latin Americans immigrate to the United States. Unlike the earlier Irish, Italian, German, and other European Catholics who immigrated to the United States accompanied by their own clergy, Latinos and Latinas continue to suffer from a severe shortage of Spanish-speaking clergy. Add to this the fact that U.S. Hispanics tend to experience the typical U.S. Catholic parish as extremely cold and impersonal, and we have the makings of a major ecclesial crisis. Indeed, thousands of Hispanics are not waiting around but are seeking out those faith communities where they do experience hospitality, vibrant worship, and a church leadership chosen from within the Latino/a community itself: in evangelical and, especially, pentecostal churches. In other words, the attraction of evangelical and pentecostal churches is that, in many ways, the *manera de ser* that Latinos and Latinas encounter there is more similar to the world of popular Catholicism, with its emphasis on relationships and physical, affective expressions of faith, than is the life of most Catholic parishes.

The challenge is thus a profound one. Given demographic trends, the future of Catholicism in the United States will be directly dependent upon the future of Hispanics in the U.S. Catholic Church. In turn, if Latinos and Latinas are to remain active in the Catholic Church, a fundamental renewal in church life is necessary. We must develop a renewed appreciation of popular forms of worship and develop creative ways of integrating popular religion with the official sacramental life of the church, so that each can benefit from the other. We must be able to link together the parish church and the domestic church more effectively. Christian history itself offers important resources for fostering such an integration. Indeed, the challenge represented by Latino/a popular Catholicism—and the challenges facing Latino/a Catholics—may contribute to a renewed appreciation of the diversity of the Christian liturgical tradition.

The roots of popular religion extend to the earliest years of the Christian community, where official and popular dimensions of Christian life were viewed as integrally related. In its earliest years, the Christian community worshiped in a variety of ways, including the shared meal and ecstatic, Spirit-filled practices that flowed in and out of the meals. So, in the Corinth of Paul's time, "Worship was focused around a shared meal and a gathering of the community in which each individual brought hymns, words, songs and various forms of ecstatic gifts."[5] Gradually during the first generations, worship became increasingly formalized, and "Paul's ecstatic and disordered gathering in which each person brought a hymn or a psalm or a spiritual experience had no part to play."[6] Though increasingly relegated to the periphery as worship became focused on formal, highly structured, clerically led worship, such forms of personalized, spontaneous, lay-identified devotion and worship continued into the Middle Ages (as noted above). In medieval Spain, for instance, while "the dominant discourse was clearly that of the Catholic Church, with its reinforcement in the liturgy," there also proliferated

> local demotic discourses [that] could take many different forms, from the language of saints and devotion to particular images, to those of spiritual powers, local healers, and debates about the role of any number of local sprites, goblins and others. . . . Each level of religious discourse clearly interacts, to a greater or lesser extent, with all the others, but need not overlap in terms of perceived contradictions or tensions. Most ordinary people can have dual or even

multi-discursive competence and can switch from discourse
to discourse depending on circumstances.[7]

Nevertheless, the very close relationship that originally existed
between eucharistic worship and more personalized, spontaneous,
and affective forms of worship became increasingly tenuous as the
former became more formalized and dominant. The latter then
became (literally) marginalized, pushed to the liturgical periphery
of the Christian community and the geographical periphery of
emerging cities in Europe. The parish churches were the centers
of what sociologist Martin Stringer calls the "dominant" liturgical
discourse, even as local shrines, popular processions, and devotions constituted a "demotic" discourse. Yet individual Christians
continued to participate in both. The dominant discourse of the
church's sacramental life was not perceived as separate from or in
conflict with the demotic discourses of local, popular devotions.
Even though the ecclesial distance between official liturgy and
popular worship had increased, the centrality of the dominant
liturgical discourse (Eucharist) never completely eclipsed the simultaneous, interrelated role that popular religion played.

An appreciation of this history would relativize the distinction
between official, formal worship and unofficial, popular worship
since these are seen as inherently intertwined from the very beginning. This approach would correct an unfortunate and unintended
consequence of Vatican II:

> Inspired by the new liturgical reforms of Vatican II, pas-
> tors and liturgists focused on a greater participation in the
> corporate liturgy, doing their best to eliminate the faithful's
> custom of performing private devotions during mass, in the
> hope that they would be more disposed to what the Church
> was now offering them. If liturgists were more attentive to
> the positive foundations of popular religiosity in the origins
> of the Church, and to its useful role in Christian life, the
> situation would have been different, but that was not the
> case. In fact, when popular religiosity entered the agenda
> of the liturgical movement, it did so in negative form, in
> competition with liturgical reforms.[8]

Contemporary liturgical theologies have tended to separate and compartmentalize what have, for most of Christian history, existed in mutual interrelation:

> The two traditions of meal and Spirit, while both being re-invigorated during the twentieth century, have yet to come together in any meaningful way. If or when they do, . . . we will see something very significant within the church and the possibility of a new round of renewal and growth of faith and practice.[9]

Indeed, the attraction of so many Latinos and Latinas to pentecostal worship may be explained—at least in part—by the common character of both Latino/a popular Catholicism and Pentecostalism as demotic, marginal discourses with common roots in the more affective, personalized forms of worship that were part of Christian liturgical life from the beginning. The same may be said of all charismatic forms of worship, Catholic or Protestant. An appreciation of the common historical roots of demotic charismatic forms of worship and the dominant eucharistic worship would contribute to an increased appreciation of the complementarity between eucharistic and Spirit-filled worship, between official and popular forms of worship. This recognition would be of particular significance to U.S. Hispanic Catholics given the dramatic growth of charismatic Catholicism in both Latin America and the U.S. Latino/a community.[10]

THE BIG STORY AND LITTLE STORIES

If the lived faith of the Christian community (what has traditionally been called the *sensus fidelium*) is the key locus of God's revelation in history, the central function of popular Catholicism as an expression of that *sensus fidelium* calls for a reexamination of the relationship between the official tradition and the popular traditions of the church—what Alejandro García-Rivera has called the relationship between the "Big Story" and the "little stories."[11] As we begin to appreciate the significance of popular religious practices in the life of the church, we can begin to appreciate more fully the role of eucharistic worship as essential and central to that life while, at the same time, resisting the tendency to reduce worship to eucharistic worship. What Latino/a popular Catholicism inherently calls into question is not so much the clericalization of the Eucharist as the "eucharistization" of the liturgy. Pecklers notes that, while the Second Vatican Council rejected such liturgical reductionism, the failure to identify popular devotions as liturgy may have contributed to a certain ambiguity in postconciliar interpretations:

> Vatican II quickly accepted the fact that the liturgy "does not exhaust the totality of the Church's activity" . . . and that the Christian community's spiritual life extends beyond liturgical participation. . . . Consequently, non-liturgical popular devotions are fostered by the Church and can, in fact, be an important instrument for evangelization, leading the faithful to the liturgy itself. . . . But precisely because popular devotions are not considered "liturgical acts," they do not introduce a separate section in the Conciliar document [*Sacrosanctum Concilium*], as is the case with the eucharist and other sacraments, the liturgy of the hours, and others.[12]

Again, this is not to suggest that the Eucharist should not be at the center or heart of the church and its liturgical life, but rather that that life should not be effectively limited to the Eucharist. Indeed, if popular traditions are allowed to engage the church's official liturgical celebrations, these might be enriched in the process. After all, the tradition is itself the product of popular traditions. "The Church and its liturgy," argues Pecklers, "have no future if they are relegated to a form and structure with a distant and exalted language, which is very far from the common people and common life. Popular religiosity makes a great contribution precisely because it is so accessible to simple and common people, in their daily lives, and confers on them the power to affirm their proper dignity and role within a broader Church."[13]

How might the life of the church be enriched if the relationship between the lived faith of the people as embodied in popular Catholicism, or in the *sensu fidelium*, and the official tradition were less unidirectional (traditions——➤popular traditions) and more truly dialectical (tradition◄——➤popular traditions). Indeed, when the Big Story no longer feeds or draws upon the little stories, the Big Story ceases to have any impact on the everyday lives of people; they are no longer willing or able to claim it as their story. When the tradition is uprooted from the popular traditions that nurture it from generation to generation, the tradition will eventually die.

A reintegration of these two intrinsically related dimensions of Christian liturgical tradition would also serve to retrieve the historical relationship between parochial and domestic practices, the church and the home. We should not forget, after all, that the original Christian place of worship was the home—and not only for practical reasons of survival. "To the extent that the central Christian ritual had its origins in the domestic context of a meal," holds Pecklers, "it continued to be celebrated in private residences for several hundreds of years. . . . Even leaving aside the fear of persecution, some Christians defended the lack of altars and sacred places, arguing that God's temple is the entire world and it could hardly be enclosed within any building constructed by humans."[14]

To recover an integral understanding of liturgy, therefore, we must resist attempts at reductionism, whether by ignoring the role of popular religious practices in the worship life of the community or by rejecting the central role of eucharistic worship. Indeed, my argument has been that only by retrieving their integral relationship can we adequately understand each of these dimensions and accord each its proper place in the community's liturgical life. As Pecklers holds (citing the work of Anscar Chupungco), "The symbolic richness and cultural traditions inherent in popular religiosity can enhance tremendously our liturgical life . . . and in this way prepare the faithful for a more active liturgical participation. On the other hand, the official liturgy can be instructive for the varied devotions in popular religiosity, as long as it makes its own contribution."[15]

Consequently, the challenge represented by U.S. Latino/a popular Catholicism is a call to the larger church to embrace once again popular religious practices as important sources of spiritual vitality and mediators of the tradition. At the same time, Latino/a

Catholics are themselves challenged to engage that tradition, especially in eucharistic worship, as the wellspring from which the little stories draw life and as the context wherein these stories will themselves inform the development of the larger tradition. To the extent that, as a truly American church, we can move toward such an integral life of worship, we will more fully incarnate Pope John Paul II's vision of *ecclesia* in America.

THE DIFFERENT HISTORIES OF NORTH AND SOUTH

To appreciate U.S. Hispanic popular Catholicism as both traditional and countercultural, we must first understand the different histories of the Catholic Church in Latin America and in the United States. The roots of Latin American Catholicism are found in Iberian medieval and baroque Christianity, whereas the roots of Anglo-Catholicism in the United States are found in northern European post-Tridentine Roman Catholicism. As historian William Christian has noted, the medieval Christian worldview and faith were not seriously threatened in Spain "until . . . the late eighteenth century."[16] Consequently, Iberian Catholicism was not forced to develop a response to the Reformers' arguments or rebut them point by point—as, also, European Catholics in the United States would later be forced to do.[17]

In order to defend itself against the Protestant threat to orthodoxy, northern European Catholicism would become increasingly rationalist, demanding a clarity, precision, and uniformity in doctrinal formulations that were simply not necessary in areas where "Catholic" and "Christian" continued to be essentially interchangeable terms; in Spain, there was no urgent need to define, clarify, and distinguish Catholic belief, especially in the wake of the *reconquista* and the expulsion of the Jews in 1492.[18] (It is no coincidence that Thomas Cajetan, a "father" of modern neo-scholasticism, was also the papal legate to Germany who, in the sixteenth century, examined Martin Luther and helped draft the papal bull *Exsurge Domine*, which condemned Luther.) It would be the more rationalist, northern European Catholicism that would take hold in the English colonies, an understanding of Catholicism that continues to inform the U.S. Catholic establishment to this day, whether conservative or liberal.

The differences between Catholicism in the English and in the Spanish colonies were reinforced by the fact that, like the Iberian colonizers as a whole, Iberian Catholicism interacted—even if often violently—with an Amerindian culture that, in many ways, shared a worldview quite similar to that of medieval Christianity. Conversely, like the English colonizers as a whole, Anglo-American Catholicism in the English colonies generally rejected any such intermingling with the indigenous culture, preferring to expel and exclude rather than subjugate and subdue that culture.

To understand our contemporary context and address successfully the challenges and opportunities of the future, therefore, the Catholic Church in the United States must begin by recognizing the fact that Catholicism in this country did not begin in the English colonies but, rather, on the shores of what is now Florida, in the deserts of what is now New Mexico, and, indeed, in the first voyages of Columbus. Without rejecting either of these histories, or any of those that came afterward in subsequent waves of immigrants, we must begin to forge a future rooted in that polyglot, multicultural past.

Drawing on his research into the historical origins of Latino/a popular Catholicism, Orlando Espín observes that the Iberian Christianity brought by the Spanish to Latin America "was medieval and pre-Tridentine, and it was planted in the Americas approximately two generations before Trent's opening session."[19] He continues: "While this faith was defined by traditional creedal beliefs as passed down through the Church's magisterium, those beliefs were expressed primarily in and through symbol and rite, through devotions and liturgical practices. . . . The teaching of the gospel did not usually occur through the spoken, magisterial word, but through the symbolic, 'performative' word."[20] Yet, in their everyday lives, Christians did not clearly distinguish creedal traditions from liturgical and devotional traditions; both were assumed to be integral dimensions of *the* tradition. Espín avers that "until 1546 *traditio* included, without much reflective distinction *at the everyday level*, both the contents of Scripture and the dogmatic declarations of the councils of antiquity, as well as devotional practices (that often had a more ancient history than, for example, Chalcedon's Christological definitions)."[21] At the grass roots, medieval culture accepted, and even encouraged, the kind of complexity that would be perceived as threatening by later generations needing to draw clear and distinct confessional boundaries: "Many of the characteristic features of medieval culture come from the cultivation of complexity, from the enchantment and the challenge represented by contradictions, from the *yes and no* as this was expounded by Abelard, the Parisian intellectual and Christian theologian of the 12th Century."[22] According to Espín, the clear distinction between dogma—that is, the content of tradition—and worship—that is, the form in which that tradition was embodied in everyday life—did not become crystallized until the Council of Trent. Espín goes on to suggest that "on this side of the Atlantic the Church was at least in its second generation, and it took approximately another century for Trent's theology and decrees to appear and become operative in our ecclesiastical scene."[23]

Liturgical theologian Mark Francis notes that

during its formative period and even after the struggle for independence from Spain, Catholicism in Latin America never underwent the systematic standardization that was brought about by the Council of Trent elsewhere in the Catholic world. North American Catholicism, for example, was largely dominated by clergy drawn from European ethnic groups who immigrated to this country along with their people in the nineteenth century and who were inspired by the norms and centralized pastoral practices of Tridentine Catholicism. In contrast, Hispanic Catholics, except perhaps those from large cities, have never been historically so influenced. The first period of evangelization of Latin America antedates the Council of Trent; and even after the decrees and norms established by the council were promulgated in Europe, their implementation was slow and sporadic, even into the nineteenth century.[24]

Its medieval roots also contribute to the peculiarly noninstitutional character of Latin American popular Catholicism. There is no doubt that popular Catholicism draws heavily from the symbolic, liturgical, and evangelical resources of institutional Catholicism and, indeed, contributes to the development of those broader traditional, official resources. (Again, the increasing popularity of devotion to Our Lady of Guadalupe beyond the borders of Mexican or even Latin American Catholicism is a prominent example.) Yet the vitality of popular Catholicism comes primarily from its intimate connection to the everyday life of the people, particularly its deep, intimate connection to domestic life. Likewise, religious leadership is not primarily male and clerical but female and lay; traditions are not passed down primarily through official ecclesiastical organs but through educational and catechetical structures that are quite tangential to the official, sacramental life of the parish. These two dimensions clearly intersect (especially in the celebration of important life events such as birth, marriage, and death), but neither are they simply coextensive.

Once again, these characteristics reflect the premodern roots of Latino/a popular Catholicism. The exclusive identification of the church with the institution, hierarchy, juridical structure, and clergy only became widespread and entrenched in the wake of the Protestant Reformation, as a defense against the challenges it presented. Avery Dulles locates what he calls this "deformation of the true nature of the Church" in the late Middle Ages:

> Catholic theology in the Patristic period and in the Middle Ages, down through the great Scholastic doctors of the thirteenth century, was relatively free of institutionalism. The strongly institutionalist development occurred in the late Middle Ages and the Counter-Reformation, when theologians and canonists, responding to attacks on the papacy and hierarchy, accented precisely those features that the adversaries were denying. . . . The institutional outlook reached its culmination in the second half of the nineteenth century, and was expressed with singular clarity in the first schema of the Dogmatic Constitution on the Church prepared for Vatican Council I.[25]

Dulles's point is reinforced by historian Gary Macy: "In the late Middle Ages, in particular, claims for control of ecclesiastical governance became more strident."[26] Prior to that, the precise character of the church and of what constitutes Christian tradition, authority, and belief was broader and less clearly defined.[27]

While in the medieval church, "there certainly was a quite distinct clerical culture with its own set of laws and rituals," among the forces that helped define medieval Christianity were the laity, religious women, and popular religious practices; these are too often ignored by contemporary historians who read back into that period our contemporary ecclesiological assumptions (e.g., that the church is identical with what we today might call the official or institutional church).[28]

The exclusion of the laity, religious women, and popular religious practices from our definition of the church in the Middle Ages served the purposes of both the post-Tridentine papacy, which argued that "the one true Church had always and everywhere agreed on the fundamental dogmas proclaimed at Trent . . . thus preserving a unified voice down through the centuries," and the Protestant Reformers, who argued that "the Roman Curia . . . used its totalitarian powers to ruthlessly enforce its heretical will."[29] Moreover, as Macy notes, "This mythology suited equally well the anti-clerical agendas of the Enlightenment and of the nineteenth century. In this scenario, religion—especially institutional religion—presented a unified opposition to science, education, and any form of liberation."[30]

In our contemporary ecclesial context, the identification of the church with the juridical structure and its official representatives has thus served the purposes (whether wittingly or unwittingly) of both Catholic neoconservatives and liberals—precisely insofar as both are operating within the framework of the fundamentally modern ecclesiology that emerged in the late Middle Ages and gained prominence in the Reformation, Trent, and Vatican I. Whether to promote or reject that ecclesiology, both neoconservatives and liberals are dependent on it. In the United States, one consequence has been that the important place of popular religion in the life of the church has been either depreciated or ignored altogether. In Latin America, the enduring force of popular Catholicism has prevented its complete marginalization. As post-Enlightenment ecclesiologies gained greater influence in the nineteenth and twentieth centuries, the Latin American Catholic Church has developed on two parallel if often overlapping levels: the popular Catholic practices that are central to the everyday lives of the vast majority of Latin American Catholics, and what many refer to as *la religion de los curas* (the religion of the priests). Precisely because this complexity retains similarities to medieval Christianity, a better understanding of medieval Christianity might contribute to a deeper appreciation of Latino/a Catholicism.

This history also helps underscore not only the similarities but also the differences between Latin American and European popular Catholicism: "Because it adhered more strictly to the spirit of the Council of Trent, the devotional life of most of the European immigrant groups . . . was regulated by the clergy, who were instrumental in its revival during the nineteenth century. Latin America never had a history of such clerical oversight, both because of a lack of native clergy and a policy toward popular religion that was much more laissez-faire on the part of the Church."[31] Thus, Euro-American popular Catholicism has a different ecclesiastical history from that of U.S. Latino/a popular Catholicism, even though they share a similar emphasis on symbol and ritual as defining the way in which the faith is lived out.

As Catholicism in the United States becomes increasingly pan-American, the historical argument of scholars like Espín and Francis becomes increasingly relevant for understanding our context both theologically and pastorally. The Catholicism that originally came to Latin America was essentially Iberian and medieval in character; the Catholicism that came to the English colonies was northern European and, as Jesuit historian John O'Malley has argued, essentially modern in character. This distinction has important ramifications. For instance, the distinction helps explain why U.S. Hispanic Catholics, being of little real interest to either liberal or conservative mainstream Catholics, are generally invisible to scholars of American Catholicism, whether these scholars are liberal or conservative; Euro-American Catholics in the United States, whether liberal or conservative, share an essentially modern worldview that tends to view Latino/a Catholicism with suspicion.

Ironically, the reasons for the suspicion are similar to those that legitimated anti-Catholic, nativist sentiments against Euro-American Catholics not long ago. In both cases, an underlying modern prejudice against anything "medieval" (the word itself so often used as a synonym for "backwardness") has engendered violent reactions against any group perceived as embodying a worldview, values, or beliefs that in any way resemble those of medieval Christianity, which are themselves perceived as naively materialistic, superstitious, and infantile:

> The United States in the nineteenth century was Protestant and revolutionary, and Roman Catholic immigrants became the enemy. . . . [Matteo] Sanfilippo points out, for instance, that it became extremely important in the nineteenth century to prove that the medieval Vikings, not Columbus, discovered America, since Columbus was "Italian, Catholic and in the service of Spain," while the Vikings were the ancestors of the nordic democratic and Protestant world. It is from this thought-world that [Protestant *and* Catholic] medievalists draw when they unwittingly and uncritically paint "the medieval Church" as a "Roman Catholic" monolith.[32]

Thus, if Irish American Catholics today are wary of Mexican American Catholics, it is because the latter embody a type of Catholicism similar to that which Irish American Catholics have long been trying mightily to live down, so as to be accepted as full-fledged members of our modern democracy. Arguing that the prejudice against medieval Christianity is based on the anachronistic assumption that medieval Christianity was identical with post-Tridentine Roman Catholicism, Gary Macy has perceptively diagnosed the problem facing Hispanic Catholics in the United States: "If the Church in the Middle Ages was tyrannical, corrupt, and immoral, and the Church in the Middle Ages was (and is) Roman Catholic, then Roman Catholics are immoral, corrupt, and tyrannical. Hispanics, as mostly Roman Catholics, can therefore be expected to be devious, immoral, lazy, technologically underdeveloped, and ignorant."[33] The irony lies in the fact that, whereas in the first half of the twentieth century, Catholics as a whole were the objects of this modern prejudice, today it is Hispanic Catholics who are often the objects of prejudice at the hands of a thoroughly Americanized, thoroughly modern U.S. Catholic establishment that has assimilated the modern prejudice against the Middle Ages.

The point here is not to suggest either that U.S. Latino/a popular Catholicism can simply be equated with medieval

Christianity, which it of course cannot, or to suggest that we can or should somehow return to some romanticized version of medieval Christianity—which was, after all, also characterized by a great deal of horrific violence, oppression, and corruption. Rather, I simply mean to suggest that, while not sufficient, an understanding of the historical influences of medieval Christianity on Latino/a popular Catholicism is certainly necessary in order to understand how Latino/a popular Catholicism functions as a source of identity, resistance, and empowerment in the Hispanic community.

"MERELY" A SYMBOL? UNDERSTANDING U.S. LATINO/A POPULAR CATHOLICISM

The medieval roots of Latino/a popular Catholicism have further implications. As Orlando Espín and other Hispanic scholars have repeatedly observed, the faith of the Hispanic people is primarily embodied and expressed in and through symbol and ritual. Yet that statement itself raises the further question: What precisely do we mean by symbol and ritual or, more precisely, what do Hispanics mean by symbol and ritual? Here, in differing notions of symbolic expression, we find the source of conflict and, hopefully, the possibility of mutual understanding and unity.

U.S. Latino/a popular Catholicism embodies an understanding of religious symbols and, therefore, of religious faith rooted in the medieval and baroque popular Catholicism first brought to the New World by the Spanish and Portuguese in the late fifteenth and early sixteenth centuries. Such an understanding differs radically from the modern notion of symbols that, I suggest, has influenced Christianity since the late Middle Ages and became normative in the wake of the Protestant Reformation, the Council of Trent, the Catholic Reformation, and the neo-scholastic theologies that reached their apex in the nineteenth century.

One of the fundamental differences between medieval and modern Catholicism is found in their different understandings of religious symbols. As the Catholic philosopher Louis Dupré has observed, the roots of this key difference can be traced back to the rise of nominalism in the late Middle Ages. Medieval Christianity had a unified, profoundly sacramental view of the cosmos; creation everywhere revealed the abiding presence of its Creator, a living presence that infused all creation with meaning. In turn, "The *kosmos* included humans as an integral though unique part of itself."[34] As the place where one encountered the living, transcendent God, all creation was intrinsically symbolic; that is, creation re-presented God, making the transcendent God present in time and space for us, here and now. That God had not made the world only to withdraw from it, leaving it to its own devices; rather, the Creator remained intimately united to creation. All creation was thus assumed to be intrinsically meaningful and intelligible by virtue of the fact that creation was graced from the beginning. The sacred would therefore be encountered, not above or outside creation, but in and through creation.

Most systematically articulated in the writings of Thomas Aquinas, this organic, sacramental worldview was reflected, above all, in the religious practices of medieval Christians. To them, matter mattered. Religious life was sensually rich; the believer encountered God in the physical environment, through the five senses. The Christian faith of the Middle Ages was firmly anchored in the body: the body of the cosmos, the body of the person, the body of Christ. Contrary to the modern stereotype of the medieval Christian as having a dualistic worldview antithetical to the human body, the Christian of the Middle Ages "assumed the flesh to be the instrument of salvation" and "the cultivation of bodily experience as a place for encounter with meaning, a locus of redemption."[35] Of course, as in every age, the view of the body was also profoundly ambiguous and conflicted.[36]

This organic, intrinsically symbolic worldview also implied a particular understanding of the relationship between the individual person and the cosmos: the person was integrally related to the rest of creation and its Creator. Knowledge of reality thus implied relationship; it is through interpersonal interaction that we could come to know God, ourselves, other persons, and creation.

According to Dupré, this organic, holistic, integral, sacramental worldview began to break down during the late Middle Ages. Afraid that too intimate a connection with material creation would compromise God's absolute transcendence, nominalist theologians such as William of Ockham effectively removed God from creation. Ineffable in being and inscrutable in his designs, God withdrew from the original synthesis altogether. The divine became relegated to a supernatural sphere separate from nature, with which it retained no more than a causal, external link. This removal of transcendence fundamentally affected the conveyance of meaning. Whereas previously meaning had been established in the very act of creation by a wise God, it now fell upon the human mind to interpret a cosmos; the person became its source of meaning.[37]

The nominalist coin had another side, however: such an understanding of God's autonomy and freedom implied the autonomy and freedom of creation itself. Paradoxically, then, the Christian attempt to safeguard God's transcendence from creation laid the groundwork for the emergence of modern rationalism and secularism. In order to protect God's immutability and transcendence, nominalism posited an absolutely inscrutable God and, as a corollary, an absolutely inscrutable creation. It was thus left up to the human subject alone to construct meaning. It would be left to theology to construct in theory a meaning that was no longer available to everyday praxis; theology would replace the lived faith (worship, praxis) as the primary locus of the Christian's encounter with God.

Likewise, neo-scholastic theologians like Thomas Cajetan began to read Thomas Aquinas through a modern, dualistic lens. Their theology "detach[ed] the realms of nature and faith from each other."[38] The birth of modern Christianity is thus characterized by the splitting, or dichotomizing of reality: as God is severed from creation, the natural and spiritual realms are separated, and, in the end, the human person—now as an autonomous "individual"—is severed from both God and nature: "modern culture . . . detached personhood from the other two constituents of the original ontological synthesis."[39] Henceforth, the autonomous individual would stand outside God, who is far removed from everyday life, and outside nature; if God is autonomous from us, then it only stands to reason that we must be autonomous from God. If, eventually, secular humanists would preach a world without

God, it was only because Christians had already been preaching a God without a world.

The breakdown of what Dupré calls the "medieval synthesis"— a worldview in which God, the cosmos, and the person were integrally related—also had important consequences for the Christian understanding of symbol. Medieval Christians had looked upon creation as intrinsically symbolic, making present its Creator in our midst. In the wake of nominalism and neo-scholasticism, however, the ultimate meaning of creation could no longer be encountered *in* creation, which could exist independently of its Creator; now meaning would have to be imputed to creation, or imposed on it from without. From without, the rational mind would impose a meaningful order on a world that itself lacked intrinsic meaning. Physical existence no longer revealed a God who lived in its very midst; now, physical existence pointed to a God who related to the world extrinsically. Creation-as-symbol became simply "an extrinsic intermediary, something really outside the reality [i.e., God] transmitted through it, so that strictly speaking the thing [i.e., God] could be attained even without the symbol."[40] The symbol and the symbolized were no longer really united; they would now have to be "mentally" united (to use Karl Rahner's phrase). If there was a relationship between God and creation, it would have to be one forged and explained by the human intellect.

The medieval Christian world had been pregnant with symbolic meaning, for the world of matter was recognized as the locus of God's self-revelation. From some time in the sixteenth century on, the world-as-symbol could only point away from itself to a God who remained impassible and aloof. Creation would no longer be a privileged place of encounter with the Sacred but a mere sign pointing elsewhere, to the spiritual realm where God resided transcendent and impassible. This historical process is described succinctly by the Latin American theologian Diego Irarrazaval:

> During the Middle Ages there is a popular religious vitality exemplified by the devotion to saints, pilgrimages, lay communal associations, movements of socio-religious renewal. . . . Beginning with the Council of Trent (16th Century) there is a greater control over popular practice and thought. In part, the

Counter-Reformation re-establishes links between the official and the popular (over against a Protestantism that rejects the religiosity of the masses). Later, with the Enlightenment and its rationalist excesses, there is a real rupture between ecclesiastical religion and the religion of the "ignorantes" with their erroneous ideas and rituals.[41]

Therefore, even as post-Tridentine Catholic theologians were making God evermore distant, the popular faith continued to reflect a stubborn insistence on God's abiding, concrete nearness to us in every aspect of life. That nearness was embodied above all in the elaborate religious symbols and, especially, the explicitly dramatic character of communal religious life that flowered during the baroque period. Thomas O'Meara describes baroque Catholicism as follows:

There was a universality in which Catholicism experienced God in a vastness, freedom, and goodness flowing through a world of diversity, movement, and order. Christ appeared in a more human way, filled with a personal love, redemptive and empowering. . . . The Baroque world was also a theater . . . Liturgies, operas, frescos, or palatial receptions were theatrical, and Baroque Christianity was filled with visions and ecstasies, with martyrs, missionaries, and stigmatics. . . . The theater of the Christian life and the kingdom of God moved from the medieval cosmos and the arena of society to the interior of the Baroque church and the life of the soul. In the Baroque, light pours down through clear windows into the church and states that God is not distant nor utterly different from creatures. God is actively present in the church and in the Christian.[42]

It is impossible for a contemporary Latino or Latina to read those descriptions without hearing resonances to the ways in which the Catholic faith is lived in our own communities. Neither the Christian medieval synthesis nor the dramatic faith of the baroque has, in fact, been completely destroyed—at least not yet. Their enduring influence can still be witnessed in, among other places, the lived faith of the Latin American and U.S. Latino/a Catholic communities.

The same deep faith in God's nearness reappears in Latino/a popular Catholicism, where dramatic reenactments like the *Via Crucis*, the *Posadas*, or the *Pastorela* serve as constant expressions of God's solidarity. It reappears in the polyphonic ambience of our churches, where angels and demons, saints and penitents, celestial stars and spring flowers are fully incorporated into our lives. Having been brought to Latin America by the Spanish, and having interacted with indigenous religions that often embodied similar beliefs in the nearness of the divine, Latino/a popular Catholicism is the embodied memory of the integral worldview, with Jesus Christ at its center, that is at the very heart of the Catholic tradition and that evolved in the Iberian Catholicism of the Middle Ages and the baroque.

THE CULTURE OF DEATH: THE SYMBOL AS COMMODITY

Once concrete symbols become mere symbols divorced from any specific, intrinsic content, their meaning is liberated from the constraints imposed by their specific, sociohistorical concreteness. So, for example, if the symbol of Our Lady of Guadalupe is understood apart from its visible concreteness in the form of the dark-skinned Lady who appeared on Tepeyac to a Nahua man, Juan Diego, she will be universalized, seen as simply one among many Marian symbols, and thereby stripped of her identification with a particular people. Such an identification in no way precludes a universal meaning, but that meaning is accessible only in and through one's own solidarity and identification with her people. If we want to discover the meaning of Guadalupe for us, we must enter into solidarity with her people.

When symbols are decontextualized or deracinated they lose their power to inspire, provoke, and transform. There is no surer way to destroy a symbol than by trying to explain it or say what it means. These tasks are, of course, perfectly appropriate and, indeed, necessary, but they must accompany, not replace the fundamental task of engaging the symbol through an active participation—that is, through the act of reception-response.

The deracination of religious symbols has had two principal consequences in contemporary theology: (1) the rationalist tendency to identify religious faith exclusively with individual assent to theological propositions (the modern danger), and (2) the subjectivist tendency to identify religious faith exclusively with purely interior, privatized, and therefore disembodied religious experience or spirituality (the postmodern danger). Each of these consequences has its conservative and liberal variants. So, for example, debates between the Catholic hierarchy and those Catholics who oppose the church's hierarchy may be seen as internecine debates between conservative rationalists who would impose a theological, rational uniformity on religious symbols and practices through the exercise of a centralized bureaucratic authority, and liberal rationalists who would also impose rational uniformity, though not by autocratic fiat but by insisting on a proper, mature, or informed theological understanding of religious symbols and practices (an understanding that, in the view of such liberals, the church hierarchy often sorely lacks). The paradigmatic example of these latter is the stereotyped militant liturgist who, with attention to the minutest detail, orchestrates the liturgical celebration, manipulating its symbols in order to thus generate a so-called meaningful religious experience.

Both the conservative and the liberal seek to impose meaning on symbolic reality from the outside. Neither trusts the people to worship God without explicit directions or instructions. Whether conservative or liberal, what is feared is the intrinsic power of the symbol itself (the appearance) as a mediation of God's own presence in our world; in short, what is feared is the Holy Spirit. As Robert Orsi notes in his analysis of the decline of Euro-American popular religion in the 1960s, liturgical reformers "insisted that if popular devotions were to remain a feature of Catholic life, they would have to be surrounded by *words*. . . . The saints and the Virgin Mary were to be reimagined in the languages of friendship, morality, or mythology, deemphasizing what the reformers considered an inappropriate and extravagant emphasis on the miraculous and the material."[43] That is, the saints and the Virgin Mary would have to be rationalized, explained to the people; symbols would be replaced by concepts. The saints and Mary were not really who they appeared to be, and who the people thus believed they were; their real meaning was extrinsic. This need to surround symbols with words also helps us understand the ongoing obsession with liturgical texts—on the part of both liberal reformers and conservative hierarchs; we must get the words right. The implicit identification of religious orthodoxy with correct texts simply reinforces the marginalization of the faith of the poor, a faith lived out not primarily through texts but through embodied relationships and practices.

Though words and texts are indeed necessary aspects of Christian praxis, the character and validity of religious practices cannot be reduced to words and texts. While the revision of liturgical texts, for instance, may be an important dimension of liturgical renewal, simply revising texts will not necessarily—in and of itself—alter religious practices. Consequently, if one looks for examples of genuine liturgical renewal in the Catholic world today, places where a vital liturgy has truly helped bring about a transformation not only of people's personal lives but also of social structures, one is not likely to find these in well-heeled, educated parishes where the congregants are theologically sophisticated and have been taught about the relationship between worship and social justice. Rather, that liturgical vitality will likely be found in poor parishes and neighborhoods, where the relationship between worship and justice, between Tabor and Calvary, is not only taught or preached but is first encountered palpably in the people's everyday lives.

While symbols and rituals give rise to thought and theological propositions (in the words of Paul Ricoeur), they cannot be simply reduced to such propositions without divesting the symbols and rituals of their power to make God present. As the primary expressions of religious faith, symbols and rituals demand theological explanation and critique, but theology can never forget its roots in the symbols and rituals that embody the lived faith. In their need to rationalize the faith, what distinguishes conservative from liberal Catholics is often simply the identity of the person authorized to impute meaning on religious symbols and rituals from without: that person may be the ecclesiastical authority or, perhaps, the theological, liturgical, or pastoral expert. What defines modernity is the dichotomy between faith and reason, between nature and supernature, between the material and the spiritual. As Orlando Espín reminds us, post-Tridentine Catholic theology (which is to say, post-Enlightenment Catholic theology) "responded to the reformers' arguments by assuming as valid many of the latter's premises."[44]

Beyond these dichotomies, then, what is called for is an integral understanding of religious faith, rooted in the lived faith as itself the paradigmatic symbol of the divine in our midst. The lived faith of the poor represents an alternative to both a naive realism that would perceive reality and truth as, in the words of Bernard Lonergan, "the already out there now real" and to a radical subjectivism that would reject a priori the very notions of reality and truth. The former would distort the symbolic character of the cosmos by simply identifying the symbol with the real, while the latter would distort that character by positing a merely extrinsic relation between the symbol and the real. The first leads to pantheism or idolatry while the second leads to rationalism or legalism.

The shift in the understanding of symbol that began in the late Middle Ages and continues until today has had repercussions in every area of human life. While the intent of that shift was to foster greater human freedom by liberating the individual from his or her intrinsic connection to and participation in the cosmos, as this had been conceived prior to the modern period, the effect has often been quite the opposite; the liberation of the symbol has had the unintended effect of making the person increasingly susceptible to social, political, and economic manipulation. The loosing of the person from his or her intrinsic relationship to the cosmos and, ultimately, to the God who is revealed in and through the cosmos made him or her increasingly vulnerable in the face of social, political, and, especially, economic forces.

Christianity's abandonment of symbolic realism has provided support for the emergence of a consumerist culture rooted precisely in the symbol as an infinitely malleable and infinitely manipulable source of value. Moreover, that abandonment has greatly diminished Christianity's ability to resist the dehumanizing elements of consumerist culture. If the churches no longer appreciate the transformative power of the symbol, Madison Avenue certainly does. If, in their desire to surround the symbol with words, Christians have mitigated the ability of symbols to compel, inspire, and convert, advertisers and marketers are adepts at promoting the consumers' identification with symbols unadorned by any words or explanations. Indeed, advertisements have become verbally sparse at the same time that they have become visually sophisticated; precisely the opposite of what has transpired in the world of Christian theology over the past five decades. (When it comes to understanding the power of symbols, Catholics could take a few lessons from Apple or Nike, for what is marketed in today's economy is not a product but an image, a symbol.)

To resist the commodification of the symbol, Christianity must retrieve a symbolic realism that reinforces "the interconnections among doctrines, symbols, and practices."[45] What is demanded is a retrieval of the intrinsic connection between the symbol (or the form) and its content, for it is only that connection that allows us to critique certain symbolic references and uses. In order to make this point, Vincent Miller recounts the following anecdote:

> Since my daughter was two years old, she has been intrigued with our nativity set. . . . She was interested in the stories that went with the figures . . . just as she was interested in the stories that went with more brightly colored figures a few feet away: a pink baby pig, a blue donkey, a honey-colored bear, and a young boy named Christopher Robin. As a theologian, I was more or less prepared to expound on the meanings of the nativity figures, but my training offered little help in addressing the fact that the narratives of God's incarnation in Jesus of Nazareth might have the same status for her as those of a silly old bear named Pooh. The problem here has to do with the context and framing of religious discourse, not with the content of that discourse itself. I'm confident that Luke can out-narrate A. A. Milne. He is not, however, given the chance, because the context of consumer culture does not construct the relationship between the two as conflict. We are certainly incited to choose, but choices are not exclusive. Choose and choose again. Jesus, Pooh, and the Lion King as well. *Gloria in Excelsis Deo! Hakuna Matata!*[46]

Note that Miller is not calling for a better or more theologically correct explanation of symbols in order to specify their meaning ("the little baby in the crib is Jesus, the Son of God"); rather he is suggesting that the range of interpretations is delimited by the symbols' practical historical context, a context that is never completely fixed, but neither is it ever completely indeterminate.

The problem is not that religious symbols no longer have any content (so that they must be explained, and can be explained in an indefinite number of ways) but that the symbols have been divorced from the practices that engendered them and through which they have continued to impact the life of the community. So, to revisit our earlier example, attempts to bring about liturgical renewal in middle-class contexts are inattentive to the inherent conflict between the eucharistic symbols of the liturgy and the consumerist context in which these are experienced practically. The Eucharist simply becomes one more symbol to be consumed (literally!) in the quest for individual fulfillment. Christian symbols are as susceptible to co-optation by consumer culture as are any others, unless Christians ground those symbols in a series of particular practices that will limit the semiotic malleability of the symbols. If the Eucharist is celebrated among immigrant laborers in a northern California vineyard, the possibility that the symbol will be co-opted so as to justify or rationalize the exploitation of immigrant labor will be greatly reduced. When one sees the image of Archbishop Oscar Romero worshipfully lifting the chalice heavenward during the eucharistic consecration and, simultaneously, watches his chest explode from the force of an assassin's bullet, no theological explanations of the eucharistic symbol are necessary.

As Miller has so persuasively argued in his analysis of consuming religion, modern Catholicism—whether conservative or liberal—has failed to offer effective resistance to the forces of consumerist capitalism precisely because it has failed to appreciate the intrinsic "interconnections among doctrines, symbols, and practices." What would make Christian faith capable of resisting those forces is not its ability to offer a different set of beliefs, a different understanding of Christian symbols (even if a more mature or informed understanding); rather, what would empower resistance would be precisely an insistence on the necessary and intrinsic interconnections among beliefs, symbols, and practices. If a symbol can mean just about anything, then it can be worth just about anything; the market will decide. Consumer culture is simply the socioeconomic manifestation of the nominalist worldview: brand names and logos have replaced the sacraments as mediators of grace. If the connection between a symbol and its referent is merely external and arbitrary, constructed through the exercise of human reason, the marketing gurus of today are but the contemporary equivalent of late-medieval scholastic theologians. Again, the problem is not that we wear Tommy Hilfiger jeans or drive BMWs but that we see absolutely no conflict between these and the Christian Eucharist; we fall in love with our cars, houses, spouses, and God—all indiscriminately. Indeed, we see no conflict between the crucifix that hangs behind the altar and the crucifix that hangs from Britney Spears's neck. It doesn't matter what the symbols mean, since such meanings are in any case purely arbitrary; what matters is that *I* have chosen them. Content and practice become irrelevant; meaning is constructed through the exercise of (arbitrary) individual choice.

Citing the work of Kathryn Tanner, Miller thus rejects the argument that the proper defense against consumer culture is a retrieval of specifically Christian symbols and practices. Indeed, such symbols and practices have become de rigeur: entertainment celebrities regularly make pilgrimages to Santiago de Compostela, and, for singles in search of a mate or simply a good time, churches have become popular alternatives to the local bar scene. "The problem," avers Miller, "is not that some coherent, holistic Christian culture has been shattered but that believers practice and use Christian doctrines and symbols in a way that prevents them from influencing their everyday social practices. They are instead engaged with habits of interpretation and use drawn from consumer culture which treat cultural objects as consumable decoration for the preexisting structures of everyday life."[47] Indeed, it is precisely decoration that is marketed; the product itself is but an afterthought to the real commodity, the brand name or image. (In this sense, the cassock worn by the young, pious seminarian may be simply one more brand or image indistinguishable from the designer-brand suits worn by investment bankers—and therefore no more countercultural.) The answer to the commodification of the symbol is not the retrieval of some putatively Christian culture but another way of relating to religious symbols.

To pit Christian culture or Catholic culture over against consumer culture (as some neoconservatives are wont to do) is already to grant the latter the victory, for such a perception of the role of Christianity in society remains blind to the ways in which consumerist capitalism simply assimilates other cultures while still allowing them their delusions of resistance. Some of the most avowedly countercultural Christians are also the most patently assimilated to the culture of wealth and power (e.g., neoconservative Protestants and Catholics who deride the evils of consumer culture while explicitly supporting the economic and political scions of that culture). In a world of commodified symbols, tradition itself can become a commodity, a decoration we take on as a marker of individual identity to distinguish ourselves from the larger, evil culture:

> The separation of the signifier and the signified sunder us from any organic relationship to our own past. History becomes a collection of dead styles that we can only plunder, not understand. . . . Neotraditionalist forms of Catholicism that repudiate the Second Vatican Council seem almost perfect illustrations of commodified nostalgia. . . . Inevitably, such "traditionalist" retrievals are not only innovative but also deeply contemporary. Fundamentalism is a thoroughly modern phenomenon.[48]

We plunder the past for symbols as readily as we plunder other cultures—even if the co-opted symbols have little transformative impact on the world around us. "Culture," Miller reminds us, "need not disdain difference. Cultural objects from global ethnic cuisines and aesthetics to the interests and concerns of contemporary lifestyle subcultures (urban black youth, gay and lesbian, evangelical Christian, and so on) provide both market segments and treasure troves of symbols that can be utilized in product design and marketing."[49] What are required, instead, are different practices that will embody and express a different understanding of the relationship between the symbols, practices, and beliefs that constitute culture. And, precisely as relational, those practices must be rooted in the present in its intrinsic relationship to the past; they cannot be simply excised from the past and inserted in the present.

Further, the growing influence of the Internet—despite its many benefits—has further weakened the links between symbols, practices, and beliefs. Religious symbols are now literally free to float around in cyberspace, unhinged from any necessary connection to time, place, or community. The consumer can browse indefinitely for symbols to download and use as screensavers or wallpaper, thereby definitively identifying himself or herself—except, of course, that those screensavers and wallpaper can always be exchanged for others at a moment's notice. It should come as no surprise, then, that despite messianic predictions that the Internet would revolutionize education and the dissemination of information, today the Internet is used primarily as a tool for marketing and for pornographic stimulation, both forms of commodification (of consumer brands in the first instance, and human bodies and sexuality in the second).

Again, the real concern here is not the content of Internet communication but the way in which a generation raised online has been conditioned to relate to symbols and images. The images that flit on and off my computer screen as I surf the Web are experienced as inherently transient, fungible, decontextualized abstractions that have no intrinsic reality until they appear on *my* screen. Moreover, there is no intrinsic connection among symbols and images except insofar as they share *my* screen, which is what gives them their meaning. Symbols no longer reveal or disclose meaning; they are inherently meaningless until they appear on my screen, where I provide a context and a meaning for them. The answer to this process of decontextualization is not to promote different, better decontextualized symbols (e.g., Christian symbols) but to raise questions about the very process of decontextualization and commodification, proposing—and embodying in our lives and practices—different ways of relating to symbols.

Decontextualized symbols, therefore, feed the individualistic soul of consumerist capitalism: "Traditions are pillaged for their symbolic content, which is then repackaged and recontextualized in a way that jettisons their communal, ethical, and political consequences."[50] Such therapeutic piracy allows us, furthermore, to pick and choose which aspects of a particular religious tradition we adopt and which we ignore: "Traditions are valued as sources of 'poetic and imaginative imagery,' while their logics, systems of doctrine, and rules of practice are dismissed for their rigidity and exclusivity. But it is precisely these connections that enable religion to inform the practice of life."[51] Again, the intrinsic inter-relationship among symbol, content (referent), and practices lend religious symbols their transformative power.

That interrelationship, moreover, sustains the communal dimension of religious symbols, rooting these in the ongoing, intergenerational lives of communities and institutions. Indeed, it is precisely the messiness and—let's admit it—outright sinful-ness that characterizes these concrete, historical contexts that has made contemporary individuals suspicious of the social structural contexts of religious symbols (read "institutional religion"). Re-ligious traditions and symbols would be attractive if only they could shed their concrete, social, historical, cultural, and therefore communal contexts. Yet those very contexts lend the traditions and symbols their subversive potential in a way unavailable to the autonomous individual consumer sitting in front of a computer screen: "Without the support of a community of shared belief, commitment hinges to a great extent on the willpower of the individual believer."[52]

When uprooted from their concrete contexts and reduced to commodities for private consumption, to satisfy the needs of the individual, symbols lose their power to transform not only social structures but also to transform the individual heart itself. Conversion presupposes confrontation and challenge, which in turn presuppose a radical critique of the self and its desires. If religious symbols are viewed merely as instruments for satisfying individual desires or needs (for meaning, identity, contentment, and so on), the possibility that those desires or needs may them-selves be disordered and in need of transformation never arises; religious faith ceases to be a response to a call from outside the self and becomes instead merely a self-projection. (This is not to say that the satisfaction of desires and needs is not one byproduct of faith.)[53]

What preserves the transformative power of religious symbols, then, is precisely their communal, public, practical, and structured character: "In the liturgy, one is not free to yawn and move on to a more interesting passage, or to decide that it is irrelevant."[54] What can be liberating is precisely the experience of engaging in a series of symbolic practices through which I come into contact with a truth that transcends my own screen. Symbolic meaning, then, is not merely something that I can change willy-nilly, depending upon my particular needs. Rather, symbolic meaning is something that can change me by introducing me to a series of relationships—across space and time—that transcend the "private space of consumption in the single-family home."[55]

POPULAR CATHOLICISM AS TRANSFORMATIVE RELIGIOUS PRACTICES

The Catholic tradition offers a multitude of resources for resisting the commodification of symbols in consumerist capitalism. The most important resource, however, is also arguably the most distinctive characteristic of Catholicism—namely, its sacramentalism:

Catholic Christianity emphasizes that the divine-human covenant is enacted within the everyday of life; *here* is where "it's at" between ourselves and God. *Here* God outreaches and engages with us. *Here* we respond as responsive partners. . . . Nothing is more significant to *what makes us Catholic* than the sacramental principle. It epitomizes a Catholic outlook on life in the world; if allowed only one word to describe Catholic imagination, we'd have to say *sacramental*. Theologian Richard McBrien writes, "No theological principle or focus is more characteristic of Catholicism or more central to its identity than the principle of sacramentality. . . . St. Augustine defined a sacrament as "a visible sign of invisible grace." The sacramental principle proposes that everything in our life-world can be such a sign. In the classic phrase of Ignatius of Loyola, Christians are invited "to see God in all things."[56]

"Sacramentality" is, of course, precisely the term used in the Catholic tradition to denote what we have been calling "symbolic realism." The sense of sacramentality is precisely what is lost when symbols are commodified, when they become means of individual self-expression rather than mediators of divine self-expression.

The sacraments, then, are simply privileged loci of grace, privileged instances of God's self-communication in creation. In the sacraments, Catholics have traditionally experienced the intrinsic interrelationship among symbol, content, and practice, for the sacraments are not mere free-floating symbols, but communal acts bound by certain structures and theological understandings developed over generations. This is not to say that even sacramental symbols cannot themselves be reduced to commodities that we shop around for like we shop for clothes, and that, like clothes that have gone out of fashion, we can exchange for others when the current symbols no longer satisfy our needs. As Catholics themselves have assimilated modern and postmodern notions of symbol, and have been assimilated into consumerist capitalist culture, they have likewise learned to relate to their religious traditions as commodities. Whether neotraditionalist or liberal, we have all learned to shop around for the right parish, Mass, or priest (i.e., where we feel comfortable and at home). Even so, the sacraments remain as reminders of a different way of relating to symbols, a different kind of symbolic practice.

Latino/a popular Catholicism also represents a different kind of symbolic practice, an instance of the Catholic sacramental imagination that has thus far been less susceptible to commodification precisely because most Latinos/as remain marginal to consumerist capitalist culture, even as marketers and advertisers strive mightily to more effectively meet the needs of this new market niche. "Popular religion corresponds with Catholic doctrine," writes Diego Irarrazaval; "through concrete reality (bread, water, everything visible) God enters into communication with and gives grace to God's community, and those signs are bearers of the response that the people give to God."[57] Yet popular Catholicism has not been sufficiently appreciated as a repository of the Catholic sacramental imagination and, thus, as a resource for resisting the decontextualized symbolic practices of the larger society. Thus, while Catholic theological aesthetics has emphasized the importance of liturgical and sacramental practice as a locus for Catholic theological reflection, relatively little attention has been paid to the place of paraliturgical practices in the broader sacramental life of the church. Much remains to be done if the church in the Americas is to fulfill the mandate, issued by the Latin American bishops at the Puebla conference over a quarter century ago, to "promote the mutual enrichment between the Liturgy and popular religion. . . . With its great symbolic and expressive richness, the religion of the people can provide a creative dynamism for the Liturgy."[58]

Latino/a popular religious practices can not only enliven the official sacramental practices of the church, but, by their very presence as the lived faith of the poor, they serve as a constant reminder of the social transformative character of all Catholic sacramental practices. "I believe," observes Diego Irarrazaval, "that the practices and celebrations [of the poor] enjoy a sacramental quality, because they are concrete signs of God's love and the love of God. . . . This sacramentality is the poor person's cry which has become a symbolic practice; ecclesial thought and life can be renewed through this sacramentality of the poor."[59] By concretely locating Catholic sacramentality on the margins of society and Church, Latino/a popular Catholicism provides a practical structure for faith that is less susceptible to co-optation.

The God of Latinas and Latinos is one whose reality is inseparable from our everyday life and struggles. In the very warp and weft of everyday life, what Hispanic theologians have called *lo cotidiano* (the everyday), God becomes known to us. For Latinas and Latinos, our faith is ultimately made credible by our everyday relationship with a God whom we can touch and embrace, a God with whom we can weep or laugh, a God who infuriates us and whom we infuriate, a God whose anguished countenance we can caress and whose pierced feet we can kiss.

The Christ of Hispanic Catholics encounters us through his wounded, bleeding, holy countenance, the *Divino Rostro* (Holy Countenance) seen on the walls of millions of Latino/a homes. He encounters us through his body, beaten and broken as it hangs lifeless from the cross. He encounters us, above all, as he accompanies us on the Way of the Cross, the innocent victim who continues to cry out to God even at the moment of deepest anguish.

In the eyes of many Hispanic Catholics, the greatest threat to true faith is not that of idolatry, the danger of mistaking a wooden statue for Jesus Christ himself, or superstition, the danger of utilizing everyday objects as a means of manipulating or controlling God. Rather, the greatest threat to true faith is the relegation of God to a distant corner of our world; the greatest threat to faith is that, by insisting that God is immaterial, absolutely transcendent and inscrutable, we will indeed end up making God immaterial—that is, irrelevant to our everyday lives. The greatest threat to faith is precisely that represented by a rationalist or spiritualist Christianity that preaches a God without a world; a Christ without a face, without a body, without wounds; a cross without a corpus.

Ours is not a watchmaker God who creates the world, winds it up, and then withdraws into some separate spiritual abode, leaving us to fend for ourselves. God does not liberate us by leaving us alone. (This is precisely what the modern understanding of freedom has become: a demand to be left alone.) On the contrary, the God of Jesus Christ liberates us precisely by refusing to leave us alone, by refusing to withdraw from any aspect of our lives, even the most insignificant or banal. The wounds, blood, and tears that cover his face and body are what make him present and, hence, real, for these are the source of our hope for ourselves, our community, our church, and our world. By accompanying us in our own crucifixion, Jesus witnesses to the truth of his resurrection as the source of life, for suffering shared is already suffering in retreat.

That resurrection is thus a resurrection into community, without which there can be no true life. Latino/a Catholicism presupposes the fundamental reality of communion as the source of life. Because we have been loved first, because we have been loved into life, we know that the self-sufficiency of the autonomous individual, the self-made man or woman, is an utter illusion. Even when life is but an ongoing crucifixion, in the compassion of a friend, in the compassion of Christ, we get a glimpse of the resurrection. For we know that what ultimately destroys the person is not physical death but abandonment—to be left alone is a fate worse than death itself. If the medieval Christian worldview posited an intrinsically symbolic cosmos, which makes present "God for us," then that worldview posited an intrinsically relational and intrinsically symbolic cosmos. The same can be said about the worldview expressed in Latino/a popular Catholicism. If our lives have meaning, it is not because we ourselves have constructed that meaning and imposed it on creation, but because we have been empowered to cultivate a meaning that we first received from others, ultimately from God, but that we help shape through our creative response to that gift—a meaning whose origins are outside ourselves, in God's creation and, especially, in those persons who have incarnated, or made present for us the concrete reality of God's abundant love.

If our relationships help give meaning and identity to our lives, so too do Jesus' relationships help define him. Consequently, to walk with Jesus is to walk with those whom Jesus loves—above all, his mother and the least of these, the communion of saints. Jesus too was loved into life. We can no more relate to him as a self-sufficient individual than we can relate to anyone else in isolation from their relationships. Because we know and trust that Jesus Christ accompanies us, we can trust that his mother and the entire communion of saints do also.

Likewise, the story of Our Lady of Guadalupe is not just about her; it is also a story about Juan Diego, the indigenous man to whom she appears (a point underscored by the Mexican people's reaction to Abbot Schulemberg's statement). The story of Our Lady of Guadalupe does not so much recount the apparition of someone to someone else; it recounts an encounter between two persons. In that encounter, as he comes to know and trust in Guadalupe's profound love for him (in a world that dehumanized him), Juan Diego comes to know and trust in his own dignity as a beloved child of God. The reality of Guadalupe's love, embodied in her desire to stay with him and accompany him, frees Juan Diego from the self-deprecation with which he first approached *La Morenita* at the beginning of the story. Juan Diego thus comes to know the truth of the Christian message because that truth has, quite literally, set him free—not in spite of but because of his bond with Guadalupe.

And it is the Mexican people, I would argue, who therefore exhibit the more traditional, premodern Catholic understanding of the symbol. They assume that if the sacred is not expressed symbolically, if it does not make itself visible, audible, and tangible, then the sacred simply disappears; it is no longer present. (Consequently, a modern secularist is simply someone who has dared to call the modern Christian's bluff, who has dared to cry out that, like the proverbial emperor, much of modern Western Christianity has no clothes.) For U.S. Hispanic Catholics, the crucified Christ, Our Lady of Guadalupe, Juan Diego, the saints, and all creation are the assurance that God is indeed here—not up in heaven or in some ethereal realm, but here in our very midst; they are the assurance that God is indeed real.

4

Historical Praxis as Christopraxis

From "God" to God

With its roots in a premodern worldview, or cosmology, U.S. Latino/a popular Catholicism maintains today the dangerous memory of the God who loved us first—the God whose offer of mercy, in the person of the crucified and risen Christ, makes conversion and justice possible. This is neither the deity of post-Enlightenment rationalism nor a mere expression of fundamentally human ideals, à la Feuerbach, Marx, Nietzsche, and Freud. Ours is not a god in quotation marks. Ours is a God who liberates and transforms us precisely because, at the very point when we are on the verge of being vanquished by the dehumanizing and deperson-alizing social forces that besiege us, this God remains at our side as the one whose abiding nearness (*se quedó*) continually reassures us that we are indeed loved. The possibility of liberation, in all its forms (social, political, economic, racial, etc.), thus depends on the credibility of this God; either the God of Jesus Christ is indeed the Way, the Truth, and the Life, or else we have no hope in our struggle against all those oppressive social forces that would deny us our humanity by denying us our right to be loved. The crucified and risen Christ's presence in the very interstices of our everyday life is the assurance that, in a world that would deny us our full humanity, we are indeed persons. His offer of mercy constitutes us as free persons. Thus, to question the credibility of this God is to question the possibility of our liberation from the oppressive forces that besiege our Latino/a communities. Ulti-mately, that is the dangerous memory which Latinos/as represent for the U.S. church and U.S. society—namely, the memory of a

God who cannot be wished away or deconstructed; a God who cannot be rationalized or reduced to a mere cultural artifact; but a God who is real and, therefore, makes demands on us (to use Metz's words).

In the previous chapter, I suggested that, to recognize the God of the poor, we must learn to see with the eyes of a truly sacramental, incarnational faith. In this chapter, I explore some of the implications of such a recognition for theological method in general, and for theological aesthetics and liberation theology in particular; insofar as Catholics are called to retrieve the sacramental worldview and faith that are central to Catholicism, and that is demanded by a theological aesthetics, Latin American liberation theologies and U.S. Latino/a theologies represent contemporary attempts to carry out precisely such a retrieval.

DO APPEARANCES DECEIVE?
THEOLOGICAL IMPLICATIONS

In his critique of contemporary notions of symbol, the U.S. Latino theologian Peter Casarella has noted

> a modern tendency to view the truth of the visible world with suspicion by conceiving of an idealized, self-contained, and logically precise theoretical screen. Or, in Husserl's words: "Immediately with Galileo . . . begins the surreptitious substitution of idealized nature for prescientifically intuited nature." In Galileo's wake, appearances of the non-idealized, "objective" world were well on their way to becoming mere appearances. . . . We moderns are still heirs to his distrust of appearances. Unless our bare perception of an event in the natural world is accompanied by a complex, *non-intuitive* explanation, we fear that we have not gotten to the bottom of things. Non-technical views are thought of as "superficial," which literally means "skimming the surface." Faith in the power of the scientific viewpoint compels us to take our distance from the appearance as appearance. If we really want to understand the world, we need an explanation that will unmask the illusion of what we perceive with our own eyes.[1]

Those of us influenced by liberationist and contextual theological methods have come to accept the modern distrust of appearances, the hermeneutics of suspicion, and the presupposition that "appearances deceive."[2] While helpful and, indeed, necessary for unmasking oppressive ideologies and social structures, such suspicion can become an epistemological absolute, as I suggested in the previous chapter, an a priori theoretical construct that itself masks rather than discloses reality; what begins as a suspicion that appearances are not real ends as a presupposition that they in fact are not. Any Christian theology, however, that assumes not only a suspicion but, in fact, a rejection of appearances as an aprioristic epistemological standpoint cannot ultimately appreciate a lived religion that presupposes the intrinsic relationship between appearance and reality, symbol and referent, form and content central to a sacramental worldview. U.S. Latino/a popular Catholicism is precisely such a lived religion. Thus, scholars expend a great deal of energy trying to get behind the symbols and rituals of popular religion, trying to understand what they really mean—something that, to the people themselves, may appear intuitively evident. As theologians, however, we have come to assume that nothing is intuitively evident; intuition cannot be trusted since it cannot get behind mere appearances. As Casarella notes, "Bare observation and effective moral action based upon a firm grasp of what is most essential about the real emerge as quaintly quixotic quests."[3]

This is not to deny the necessity of hermeneutical suspicion, the need to question the power interests underlying the promotion of particular religious symbols, practices, or ideologies. Nevertheless, the very principles of hermeneutical suspicion ought to be applied to the practice of hermeneutical suspicion itself; the practice of deconstruction should itself be deconstructed. Once appearance (i.e., symbol or form) and reality (i.e., the symbol's referent, what the symbol symbolizes, or the form's content) are thus separated or deconstructed, the theological enterprise is quickly reduced to the methodological task of developing the appropriate intellectual instruments for demonstrating and analyzing that separation. As important as that task is, however, when the theological enterprise is simply reduced to methodology, the possibility that appearances may in fact disclose the real is precluded a priori:

Once the differentiation of a methodological standpoint
is taken as an adequate substitute for what Lonergan calls
"the mutual enrichment" of common sense by the self-
disclosure of God, then method's edifice of a purely reflective consciousness becomes idolatrous. Taken as an end in
itself, methodological reflection—no matter how rigorous
and self-correcting—obscures the appearance of truth. When
method dominates without attention to the disclosure of
truth, theology suffers.[4]

Indeed, when method dominates, the very possibility of disclosure, as the appearance of the real, is itself precluded from the
outset; we can spend our entire lives deconstructing the appearances without ever, in fact, getting behind them. The postmodern
assertion that there is nothing at all behind the appearances—there
is no there there—appears as simply the logical conclusion of the
modern separation of the appearance and the real.

Ultimately, then, the reduction of theology to methodology
absolves the theologian of ever having to commit to a particular
truth, or to any truth at all, as that which encounters us in history,
makes an ultimate claim on our lives, and demands total commitment. Insofar as any truth can be affirmed, it will necessarily be
only an abstract truth that, because it is not intrinsically linked to
a particular appearance, symbol, or form, is presumed to have an
existence independent of such concrete symbols or forms. Thus,
underlying the separation of symbol and referent is a fundamental
distrust of particular, physical, concrete existence as disclosive of
reality; the postmodern emphasis on particularity is ultimately a
neo-gnostic denial of the unity of appearance and reality.

Conversely, any religious faith that assumes that what presents
itself as true may in fact be true will be either dismissed outright
or politely tolerated as the simple (read "naive") faith of the
people. Scholars may suggest that if the people really understood
what is behind their religious practices, what their symbols and
rituals really mean, they would know that their real concern is
not God, or Jesus Christ, or Guadalupe, or Juan Diego, but the
universal human need for cultural identity or human dignity or
liberation or self-empowerment, all of which could just as easily

be expressed—and are, in fact, expressed—in a myriad of other forms, other rituals, other religions.

Consequently, what was perplexing was not that the Mexican people could believe that Juan Diego was indeed a reality (since all of us have our own realities), but that their belief in that reality could compel them to put their very bodies and lives on the line. What was incomprehensible was not their belief as such but their conviction that that belief is a truth that makes practical demands on us. The reaction to the Mexican people's anger was to smile sympathetically while, nevertheless, assuming that whether or not Juan Diego is real ultimately does not matter; what matters is the people's belief in Juan Diego, since it is the belief that is empowering and liberating; the belief makes Juan Diego real. It is not Juan Diego who matters; what matters is what he represents or points to—for example, the value of indigenous culture and *mestizaje*, the dignity of the poor. Yet the undeniable fact is that, for the people themselves, what matters most is precisely the reality of Juan Diego—hence their reaction to the abbot's statement. What matters to them are not the values that Juan Diego represents; what matters is Juan Diego himself. While contemporary theologians may be interested in what the people's beliefs and practices mean, the people themselves understand that meaning as tied inextricably to the reality which they have encountered, the truth and credibility of the God who is near. If that God is not real, if Christ is not crucified and risen, then their beliefs and practices have no meaning since their hope would be in vain. It is to the truth of their God that the lived faith of the poor ultimately attests and on which its meaningfulness depends. In other words, to appreciate Latino/a popular Catholicism, we must bear in mind the classical Thomistic dictum: "*Actus credentis non terminatur ad enuntiabile, sed ad rem*" (The act of faith does not end in what is pronounced, but in the object).[5]

The vehemence with which the Mexican people rose up to defend Juan Diego (and with which Jesús rose up to defend the Gospel, as I related in the Introduction to this book) points, moreover, to a further problem presented by the separation of symbol and referent, or form and content, and the consequent absolutization of theological method: in the wake of that separation, it becomes difficult, if not impossible, to conceive of the true, or the real, as anything but a mere human construction, fundamentally a human product rather than a divine gift. (Hence, the modern separation of symbol and referent leads inexorably to the postmodern deconstruction of the self-as-mere-appearance; there is no substantive "self.") The symbol becomes, not the disclosure of a truth that we receive and which demands a response, in which act of reception-response we find meaning; rather, the symbol is itself the way in which we construct meaning for ourselves, the way in which we literally constitute ourselves and our world. Yet, in the words of Thomas Merton, "If reality is something we interpret and act on to suit our own concept of ourselves, we 'respond' to nothing."[6] Thus, rather than understanding the construction of meaning as necessarily linked to the disclosure of truth, to revelation, truth-as-disclosed is simply reduced to meaning-as-constructed, and the truth question is elided altogether. The symbol is not itself a disclosive and transformative real presence. Thus, it should not matter to the Mexican people whether Juan Diego is real or not, since, after all, it is not Juan Diego himself who is real but our belief in Juan Diego as a sign that we ourselves have produced over the course of generations in order to construct meaning for ourselves. Juan Diego is merely an instrument, a vehicle for constructing and conveying that meaning. What matters is not Juan Diego but ourselves, our own need for identity, our own sense of dignity, our own need for hope and liberation.

While this need is a necessary aspect of the faith of the people, it is clearly not sufficient to explain the people's own understanding of their faith. We cannot simply dismiss politely the Mexican people's reaction to the abbot. We must begin to ask whether Juan Diego and Guadalupe—and Jesus Christ—matter not just because of what they "represent," but because they are who they say they are; whether Jesus Christ himself saves us, or whether he merely represents a good person. If the latter is the case, then we save ourselves insofar as we emulate Christ's example of the good life. If the content of revelation (the "what") is not intrinsically related to the particular form of revelation, then the form itself (the person of Jesus Christ, or Juan Diego, or Guadalupe) is relativized precisely as revelation, as the inbreaking or irruption of the real in our world. Religion is then reduced to infinitely interchangeable symbols and rituals, all of which can be used as instruments or vehicles to convey meaning, to represent some value.[7]

The poor do not find meaning and hope in the religious practices *themselves*, but in the particular person of Jesus Christ, Guadalupe, and so forth. Belief alone does not save; what saves is the object, or content of that belief, that in turn evokes a practical response on our part. If Christ is not crucified and risen, our hope—the hope of the poor—is in vain.

Our inability to appreciate the character of lived faith and, specifically, lived Catholicism as a praxis of reception-response to a gift whose very particularity, historicity, and physicality prevent us from easily separating what it is from what it means results is an inability to affirm the normativity of that gift and, therefore, of any claims it might make (e.g., for social justice). Quite simply, the question of truth is reduced to a question of either meaning or usefulness: Is the faith of the poor meaningful for them? Does it work for them? Does it liberate? Out of a genuine concern for the liberation of the poor, we may be tempted to interpret popular religion through our own lenses, from the perspective of our own questions (e.g., "Does it liberate?"). In so doing, we may miss important elements of what God is trying to say to us today through the witness of the poor. Here we might heed Pope John Paul II's observation about the dangers of functionalist readings of Christian faith: "The dogmatic pragmatism of the early years of this century, which viewed the truths of faith as nothing more than rules of conduct, has already been refuted and rejected; but the temptation always remains of understanding these truths in purely functional terms. This leads only to an approach which is inadequate, reductive and superficial at the level of speculation."[8]

When we are encountered by Christ, contends Gustavo Gutiérrez, "We discover where the Lord lives and what the mission is that has been entrusted to us."[9] Thus, for the poor, liberation depends precisely on the truth, the reality, of the body of Christ and its claims. If those claims are true, if Jesus Christ was crucified and raised from the dead, if *La Morenita* did appear to Juan Diego, then everything else follows from that truth, because the truth itself saves and liberates us by con-forming us to itself, by drawing us into a participation in its own life. Our very identity is not achieved, but is given us by that truth, by the Word, which itself overpowers us.

The source of strength and liberation is not the *Via Crucis* itself, not the values behind this religious ritual, but the God of Jesus Christ, the God whose Son suffered torture and crucifixion for us, and so continues today to suffer torture and crucifixion with us. For the *abuelitas*, what empowers and liberates is not the *experience*, not the ritual or the performance or the symbols, not the meaning behind the symbols, but *God*, and not just any god but *this* God, the God whose Son conquers death by dying on the cross, the God who dies accompanied by his sorrowful mother. "To profess 'this Jesus,' to acknowledge 'Jesus the Christ,'" argues Gutiérrez, "is to express a conviction. It is not simply putting a name and a title together; it is an authentic confession of faith. It is the assertion of an identity: the Jesus of history, the son of Mary, the carpenter of Nazareth, the preacher of Galilee, the crucified, *is* the Only Begotten of God, the Christ, the Son of God."[10] "If we believe in Jesus as the Son," avers Sobrino, "it is because in him the truth and love of the mystery of God have been shown in an unrepeatable form, and been shown in a way that is totally convincing to a crucified people who have no problem in accepting Jesus' unrepeatable relationship with God so that they can confess him to be in truth the Son of God."[11]

If our praxis is liberating, it is only because it affirms something that is true. As Sobrino insists, "The resurrection of the one who was crucified is *true*. Let it be foolishness, as it was for the Corinthians. But without this foolishness, because it is true—or without this truth, because it is foolish—the resurrection of Jesus will only be one more symbol of hope in survival after death that human beings have designed in their religions or philosophies. It will not be the Christian symbol of hope."[12] For the poor, the resurrection is not merely the assurance of life after death; it is, above all, the assurance of life before death.[13] Because Jesus lives, we can dare to live. Either Jesus Christ lived, died, and conquered death for us, or he did not. Either he is the Way, the Truth, and the Life, or he is not. Either he accompanies us in our struggles today, or he does not.

The luxury of avoiding the question of truth is one accorded those of us who spend our time in the comfort of our offices, libraries, and homes; it is not a luxury available to a mother watching her child dying of hunger, or burying a child who was just caught in gang crossfire. Only our comfort, security, and affluence allow us to avoid questions of truth. Our ease of life allows us to wait around until all the data are in before ever having to answer the question, "Is it true?"—not just in a disinterested way, but as a question whose answer makes ultimate demands on our lives.

Like Peter, who, after Jesus was arrested and taken to Caiaphas, followed Jesus "at a distance" and "sat with the guards to see the end" of Jesus' interrogation before Caiaphas (Matt. 26:58), I can too easily become accustomed to observing the interrogation of Jesus from a distance, waiting until all the data are in, until the exegetes, sociologists, literary critics, and postcolonial theorists have rendered their verdicts before daring to render mine. Too often I remain content to merely observe from a distance as Jesus is put on trial and his testimony is dissected and deconstructed—until, that is, I find myself confronted by the cross; until I am confronted by the poor, in whom Christ continues to be crucified today.

Christ on the cross does not have the luxury of avoiding the truth question until all the evidence is in. Indeed, against all the available evidence, he remains resolute in his faith: "My God, my God, why have you abandoned me?" Confronting death daily, the poor do not have the luxury of postponing an answer to the truth question until all the evidence is in. A dying person does not have the luxury of observing Jesus' trial from a distance; he or she is faced squarely with a decision between belief and despair—not just belief in general, or in the abstract, but belief in either *this* or *that*, belief in either Jesus or Caiaphas. For the dying person, the difference between the "this" and the "that" is precisely what matters most; it is all that matters. To the hungry person, the truth of Christ's claims about himself is much more than an academic issue to be debated and deconstructed by exegetes and theologians. If I take that hungry person seriously, then, so too must I be willing to render a verdict on those claims. Am I willing to stake my own life on those truth claims? If I take the faith of the *abuelita* seriously, that is, if I truly respect her, I must eventually render my own verdict on her statement, "*se quedó*" (she stayed)—whether that verdict is positive or negative. The *abuelita* has certainly rendered her verdict. Will I engage that verdict, *se quedó*, or will I ignore it, pretending that, after all, it doesn't matter whether the *abuelita*'s verdict is correct or just naive . . . whether Juan Diego "is a reality"? To refuse to render my own verdict while reinterpreting hers in order to make it more theologically acceptable, in order to get behind the appearance to understand what it really means, even if with the best of intentions, is in fact to patronize her: "Isn't it quaint how she really believes all those things," even though, as all of us so-called mature believers know, whether all that stuff is actually true is not really the important thing (hence, also the importance of critical reflection as itself a necessary aspect of the option for the poor, a necessary dimension of solidarity with and respect for the poor).

As embodied in U.S. Latino/a popular Catholicism, the faith of the poor demands from us that we stake our own existence on a reality, a truth that is not reducible to abstract notions of love, justice, or freedom, but that irrupts in our world in the form of the cross, thereby subverting and overturning our own conceptions of love, justice, and freedom. It demands, moreover, that we understand the act of receiving a gift, or giving thanks, as indeed an act, as praxis. Such a contemplative faith stance becomes increasingly difficult, however, in a society in which we are taught from childhood that to be fully human we must be able and willing to grab, to grasp, to acquire.

Yet this is not at all the understanding of freedom embodied in Latino/a popular Catholicism, where freedom involves the capacity for receptivity, a capacity for responding to an other. The ability to receive is precisely what empowers one to act. Because we are indeed accompanied by the crucified and risen Christ, we have the courage to go on. Thus, for the poor themselves, the question of truth is essential. Unless Jesus Christ is the definitive form of God's love, then Jesus Christ is but one among many possible forms of love, which is then reduced to an abstract concept to be clothed in interchangeable forms. Jesus, then, is not the one who empowers us by accompanying us in our struggles.

Whether or not Jesus Christ was truly raised from the dead is not an issue of secondary importance, ultimately reducible to some general affirmation of the ultimate goodness of life; whether or not Our Lady of Guadalupe actually appeared to Juan Diego is not an issue of secondary importance, ultimately reducible to some general affirmation of God's love for the poor; whether or not the dead are raised is not an issue of secondary importance, ultimately reducible to some general affirmation of the indestructibility of life, or a belief that our ancestors live on in our memories—though, of course, all that is true. But it is true *because* Jesus Christ was raised from the dead.

Moreover, to affirm the centrality of the Word as a unity of symbol and referent is by no means to preclude pluralism; on the contrary, this affirmation is itself demanded by the truth of the cross. Authentic pluralism and dialogue preclude either an abstract universalism or an abstract relativism, both of which deny the reality of the particular as itself a precondition for pluralism and dialogue; both an abstract universalism and an abstract relativism represent fundamentally gnostic denials of the necessarily material character of revelation. Universalism and relativism are equally abstract, ahistorical denials of the sacramental principle, the assertion that the universal is necessarily mediated by the particular. Authentic dialogue presupposes that each participant make normative truth claims. Where religion is incapable of making normative truth claims, religious faith will be reduced to a matter of personal taste. (And there is no point in discussing matters of personal taste, since these are purely subjective: "I'm OK, you're OK.") The truth of the crucified and risen Christ is absolutely incompatible with any attempt to coerce or impose belief, precisely because that belief is a response to God's offer of reconciliation.

Insofar as the preferential option for the poor calls us to read the Gospel through the eyes of the poor, it subverts all our attempts to deconstruct that Gospel, to spiritualize or privatize it, to reduce it to a literary text, to reduce it to a helpful but ultimately nonessential guide for praxis, to reduce it to a matter of personal taste. The preferential option for the poor thus calls us to apprehend and embrace the crucified and risen Christ revealed in history, in the Eucharist, in the visible church, and in the church's Scriptures, as the one who invites us to participate in his life. To participate in Christ's life is to do so wholeheartedly and singlemindedly. The demands he makes of us are absolute; they call for a commitment of our whole life, in its full integrity. And we will only respond to that demand if we can embrace it as in fact true—not just meaningful, helpful, or empowering, but true—and if we can do so with the sense of urgency of those persons in our midst who confront death on a daily basis.

As Gutiérrez reminds us, Jesus asks his disciples and asks us, "Who do *you* say that I am? You; not the others. . . . What is asked refers to an objective reality, something exterior to the disciples. . . . The question pulls us out of our subjective world and, 'turning us inside out,' locates the point of reference of our faith, and of our life, beyond ourselves, in the person of Jesus."[14] And the question, "Who do you say that I am?" demands not a theoretical answer but an integral answer; we answer that question with our whole lives.[15] Scholars might prefer the more abstract questions, "Who do people say that I am? Who do the crowds say that I am?" But the crucified and risen Lord confronts each of us with the much more demanding question, "Who do *you* say that I am?"

Ultimately, the lived faith of the poor calls us to conversion. If I want to understand popular Catholicism, I must allow myself to be transformed by the same God who accompanies the community on the *Via Crucis*, by his mother, who stayed. The poor themselves have no interest in popular Catholicism; most have never even heard the term. It is not popular Catholicism that they look to for hope; they look to the Crucified; they look to his mother; they look to the saints. Can all of us allow ourselves to be illumined by that light? "It is not the same thing merely to treat things scientifically and doctrinally," holds Sobrino, "as really to shed light on them. It is not the same thing to speak of many things as to allow things to speak for themselves."[16] But, of course, that presupposes that those things really do exist and are not merely social, cultural, or literary constructions or conventions. "Theology," argues Sobrino, "must allow God to speak."[17]

If taken seriously, then, the faith of the people overturns contemporary theological assumptions, not by proposing dramatically new theological truths, but by making present on the margins of our society and church centuries-old, long-forgotten truths—indeed, by refusing to surrender the very question of truth itself. With Jon Sobrino, the faith of the people challenges us to ask the following questions:

Is there anything that is ultimate and incapable of being manipulated, anything that makes an ultimate demand on human beings in the form of promise and fulfillment? Is there anything that will prevent us from relativizing everything, reducing everything to a lowest common denominator in terms of value, although perhaps without our knowing why we should not make such a reduction? Is there anything that makes a total demand on us—anything to remind us that despite the ideals of a consumer society, despite the growing preoccupation with material security and a life of self-centeredness, as we find for example in many places in the First World, there is after all a "something else," and a "someone else," and not just as a factual datum, but as a "something" and a "someone" in terms of which we either succeed or fail in our own self-fulfillment?[18]

Latino/a popular Catholicism embodies a dangerous memory of suffering that I dare not confront because it forces me to do what years of studying and writing about theological method, hermeneutics, and epistemology have made it possible for me to avoid doing, namely, answer the questions Sobrino poses. In short, the faith of the Latino/a community calls for a new *ressourcement*, one born not in the *aulas* of Le Saulchoir and Fourviére but in the *barrios* of New York City, Chicago, and Los Angeles; in the *favelas* of São Paulo and Rio; and in the *barriadas* of Lima and Mexico City. The faith of the people calls for a *ressourcement* from the margins, a retrieval of the wounded yet glorified body of Christ as the locus of theology. It is a faith that, with Georges Bernanos, reminds us that "our church is the church of the saints" and that "we must seek the true cause of our misfortunes in the disincarnation of the Word."[19] The late Henri Nouwen already noted this a number of years ago when, reflecting on his experience working alongside Gustavo Gutiérrez in the slums outside Lima, Nouwen observed as follows:

> As one who has been exposed to many styles of theological liberalism, I am struck by the orthodoxy of this Christ-centered spirituality. . . . The Christians of Latin America, as Gustavo himself once pointed out to me, came to a real-

ization of the social dimensions of their faith without going through a modernistic phase. He used Archbishop Romero as a striking example. Through his direct contact with the suffering people, that traditional churchman became a social critic without ever rejecting, or even criticizing, his traditional past. In fact, Archbishop Romero's traditional understanding of God's presence in history was the basis and source of his courageous protest against the exploitation and oppression of the people of El Salvador.[20]

A Latino/a *ressourcement* would retrieve the sacramental understanding of the unity of symbol and referent as itself a dangerous memory that calls for and makes possible courageous protest. In so doing, the faith of the poor will eventually force us all to take a stand, to declare, "*This* I believe; on *this* I am willing to stake my life." Then and only then will we be liberated, freed to commit ourselves wholeheartedly to struggle alongside the God who stays with the victims of history, the God whose nearness inspires in the Latino/a community an invincible hope against hope. Insofar as our own praxis is conformed to God's cruciform praxis in history, we can become participants in the historical struggle for liberation. Only then will our theological reflection avoid devolving into a "reading without repentance, knowledge without devotion, research without the impulse of wonder, prudence without the ability to surrender to joy, action divorced from religion, learning sundered from love, intelligence without humility, study unsustained by divine grace, thought without the wisdom inspired by God."[21]

CRITICAL REFLECTION ON CHRISTIAN PRAXIS IN THE LIGHT OF THE WORD

The modern and postmodern separation of the real from its particular, concrete historical form is—I would submit—alien to the lived faith of the poor and, specifically, alien to Latin American and U.S. Latino/a popular Catholicism. Consequently, the preferential option for the poor itself demands that the theologian reject such a separation. Too often, Latin American and

U.S. Latino/a theologies have been read and interpreted within a liberal-conservative ideological framework that locates these theologies within the liberal camp. Indeed, I've often heard the terms "liberation theology" and "liberal theology" used interchangeably. A consequence of such a reading is precisely that the central salvific significance of the crucified and risen Christ is depreciated (since the assertion of truth claims is assumed to be a characteristic of conservative theologies).

As elaborated by liberation theologians like Gustavo Gutiérrez, the option for the poor implies and presupposes an intrinsic connection between symbol and referent, between the real and the appearance, between the true and its disclosure. That unity is embodied in the Word of God, the crucified and risen Christ. Inspired by the work of Gutiérrez and other Latin American theologians, U.S. Latino and Latina theologians have sought to incarnate the theological method of Latin American liberation theology in the sociohistorical context of the U.S. Hispanic community—that is, we have sought to articulate a theology that takes as its starting point a preferential option for the marginalized community of Latinos and Latinas in the United States. Like Latin American liberation theology, U.S. Hispanic theology thus represents an understanding of the theological task as, in the well-known phrase of Gutiérrez, "critical reflection on Christian praxis in the light of the Word,"[22] more specifically, a critical reflection on the Christian praxis of our U.S. Hispanic communities in the light of the Word. Such a reflection has surfaced several themes that distinguish the praxis of U.S. Latino/a communities as marginalized communities. Two such central themes, for instance, are the experience of *mestizaje* and popular religion.

In the remainder of this chapter, I focus on this latter theme, popular religion—and, more specifically, popular Catholicism—to suggest that, as a defining characteristic of U.S. Hispanic Christian praxis, the faith of the people, or the lived religion of the poor, itself represents a challenge to our own theologies and, indeed, to all theologies grounded in a preferential option for the poor, particularly those Christian theologies that understand themselves as "critical reflection on Christian praxis in the light of the Word." The faith of the people calls us to an intellectual and religious conversion that subverts the very foundations of the Christian theological enterprise as most of us have known it in modern or postmodern Western cultures. What I thus suggest is that U.S. Latino/a popular Catholicism, the lived religion of the poor, is ultimately incomprehensible for those of us schooled in modern and postmodern theological methods, unless we ourselves are converted to a radically different way of seeing.

By emphasizing the significance of popular Catholicism precisely as a central aspect of Christian praxis—that is, as a defining characteristic of the praxis of the poor—U.S. Latino and Latina theologians have broadened and deepened the understanding of praxis beyond the more explicitly sociopolitical understanding of Christian praxis emphasized in the early years of Latin American liberation theology. Indeed, Latin American liberation theologians themselves increasingly embraced this broader understanding, giving more attention to popular religion, the lived religion of the poor, as a praxis that grounds theological reflection. Thus, Christian praxis is understood to include not only sociopolitical action but also the lived faith, spirituality, ritual practices, and devotional life that, together with the struggle for social justice, are necessary, intrinsically interrelated dimensions of Christian discipleship.

Hence, as critical reflection on Christian praxis in the light of the Word, the theological enterprise always stands under the judgment of that Word—that is, theology and praxis must conform to the Word, for the latter is the foundation of both theological reflection and praxis. "'God first loved us' (1 John 4:19)," writes Gutiérrez, and he continues,

> Everything starts from there. The gift of God's love is the source of our being and puts its impress on our lives. . . . From gratuitousness also comes the language of symbols. . . . In their religious celebrations, whether at especially important moments or in the circumstances of everyday life, the poor turn to the Lord with the trustfulness and spontaneity of a child who speaks to its father and tells him of its suffering and hopes. . . . The other is our way for reaching God, but our relationship with God is a precondition for encounter and true communion with the other.[23]

The poor and excluded understand that, before we can choose God or others, God has already chosen us. Christian praxis is, at bottom, a praxis of grateful reception and response; before praxis is the action of a historical agent, the action of a recipient; before it is action-as-doing, it is action-as-receiving. More specifically, we become historical agents precisely in the praxis of reception and response. "God first loved us. . . . Everything starts from there." Our openness to and reception of God's love is the precondition for any truly liberative praxis; the latter is but the eucharistic, or grateful response to the former.[24]

The increased attention to popular religion *as praxis*, as the starting point of theology, brings to light those aspects of Gutiér-rez's method too often underappreciated in the past, namely, the specifically *Christian* aspects of his definition of theology: "*critical* reflection on *Christian* praxis in the light of the *Word*." That is, Jesus Christ is himself intrinsic to theology and praxis; the life of faith itself has a transcendent source, the Word. The doing of theology, the struggle for justice, and the life of prayer are all necessary and intrinsically interrelated dimensions of our response to Jesus Christ, the One who loved us first and whose preexistent love compels our response. In other words, it matters that Jesus Christ is real because he is the One who elicits and makes possible our theological reflection, our work for justice, and our worship. We cannot do Christian theology unless we assume that Jesus Christ is who he says he is—"the Way, the Truth, and the Life"—since theology and faith are but a response to the crucified and risen Christ who loved us first.

In this sense, Gutiérrez's understanding of human action reflects that of John Paul II in his encyclical letter *Veritatis Splendor*, where he defined the moral life as "the response due to the many gratuitous initiatives taken by God out of love for man. It is a response of love. . . . Thus the moral life, caught up in the gratuitousness of God's love, is called to reflect his glory."[25] When Christ looks at us, smiles, and calls out our name, we must respond. When *La Morenita* calls out Juan Diego's name, he must respond. The entirety of liberation theology is rooted in that response.

Interpreting liberation theology as a liberal theology, however, leads one to underestimate the significance of the adjective in the phrase "*Christian* praxis" and, especially, the significance of the last phrase "in the light of the Word." Gutiérrez writes,

> A hasty and simplistic interpretation of the liberationist perspective has led some to affirm that its dominant, if not exclusive, themes are commitment, the social dimension of faith, the denunciation of injustices, and others of a similar nature. It is said that the liberationist impulse leaves little room for grasping the necessity of personal conversion as a condition for Christian life. . . . Such an interpretation and criticism are simply caricatures. One need only have contact with the Christians in question to appreciate the complexity of their approach and the depth of their spiritual experience.[26]

What lies behind the "hasty and simplistic interpretation" that Gutiérrez criticizes is precisely the assumption that for liberation theologians "truth" is simply a human construction; it matters little what one believes as long as one is committed to the struggle for justice. Christ would then be not the one who makes that commitment and struggle possible but merely one among many role models we can look to as we engage in the struggle. Gutiérrez says that theology is a second step, not that Christ is a second step.

What grounds theology is not praxis as such but praxis as encountered by God's Word: "The ultimate criteria come from revealed truth, which we accept in faith, and not from praxis itself. It is meaningless—it would, among other things, be a tautology—to say that praxis is to be criticized 'in the light of praxis.'"[27] Such an acceptance in faith always implies a total commitment of the whole person; it implies a praxis of faith whose "inescapable context" is "the massive social, economic, and political marginalization of the majority of the earth's people."[28] In the act of solidarity with the poor, the truth of God's Word in the person of Jesus Christ is revealed.

When we opt for the poor, we are confronted with a paradox: the more profoundly we accompany the poor, the more profoundly we identify with the Christian praxis of the poor and reflect critically on that praxis in the light of the Word, the more we are confronted with a lived faith that takes as its starting point, not praxis per se, but the gratuitous Word of God, Jesus Christ himself (including the entire communion of saints at whose center Christ stands). As received by us in and through our lives of discipleship, our lives of Christian praxis, the gratuitous Word of God is "a precondition for encounter and true communion with the other." In Gutiérrez's words, "Everything starts from there." That is, the more we look to the poor, the more they compel us to look to God and what God has done and continues to do for them and for us: "the gratuitousness of God's love is the framework within which the requirement of practicing justice is to be located."[29] Irarraza-val notes how his work among the poor of Peru has deepened his understanding of the meaning of liberation:

> I should confess that ten years ago I used a measuring rod with two poles: oppression and liberation. The people have been teaching me to see more colors and broaden my criteria. . . . Like the people say, "with faith, anything is possible," and "we are fine, thanks be to God." It seems to me that this logic of reciprocity, expressed in the ritual celebration that transforms conditions of impoverishment and that infuses hope is how a great part of the people understand the theology of liberation.[30]

Before we look at Christ, he has already looked (smilingly) at us.

Our ability to act as historical agents, our freedom, our very identity are themselves given us by the God who loved us first, the God who is fully revealed in the wounded body of the crucified and risen Christ, in his mother, in the communion of saints. Like Gutiérrez, Jon Sobrino explains very clearly that a genuine solidarity with the poor is always a response to God's own loving call:

> To be encountered by the Lord is the experience of the love of God. Indeed it is the experience of the fact that love is the reality that discloses to us, and makes us able to be, what we are. It is God's coming to meet us, simply because God loves us, that renders us capable of defining our very selves as who we are, in order, in our turn, to go forth to meet others. . . . Without a true encounter with God, there can be

no true encounter with the poor. . . . To have genuine love
for our sisters and brothers, we must have an experience of
the God who first loved us.[31]

The preferential option for the poor accords a privileged status
to the faith of the poor and in so doing paradoxically redirects
our attention from that faith itself to a divine praxis that is the
source of our own experience, the source of our own praxis, the
source of our own life. The grounds for the preferential option
for the poor, then, are ultimately theological (not methodological
or even epistemological). "The ultimate basis of God's preference
for the poor," argues Gutiérrez, "is to be found in God's own
goodness and not in any analysis of society or in human compassion, however pertinent these reasons may be."[32] Our ability to
recognize, receive, and embrace, in the crucified and risen Christ,
the concrete, unrepeatable form of God's love as the source of
our very identity is inseparable from the ability to embody that
love in our social praxis; these are two inseparable dimensions
of Christian praxis as a praxis of reception and response. "The
good which God does to us," writes Aidan Nichols (drawing on
Hans Urs von Balthasar), "can only be experienced as the *truth*
if we share in *performing* it (John 7:17; 8:31ff.); we must '*do the
truth in love*' (Ephesians 4:15) not only in order to perceive the
truth of the good but, equally, in order to embody it increasingly
in the world."[33]

To speak of the act of faith as a reception and response may
be belaboring the obvious. The principal influence for many contemporary theologians, however, has been modern praxis-based
or postmodern contextual methodologies. These methodologies
have not only taken historical praxis as their starting point but,
at times, have presupposed a particular, modern Western definition of praxis as autonomous agency, itself often understood
instrumentally. (I have elsewhere argued that even the postmodern
deconstruction of the agent-subject presupposes what it claims
to reject.)[34] Praxis-based and contextual methodologies have, of
course, revolutionized Christian theology by demonstrating not
only the ethical but also the methodological and epistemological
necessity of a preferential option for the poor; the perspective of
the poor and marginalized, of the crucified people, provides a privi-

leged insight into reality. These methods have also underscored the necessarily sociopolitical dimension of our response to God's gratuitous love. What I would now like to suggest, however, is that the option for the poor is itself short-circuited and, indeed, distorted when it is not undertaken, as Gutiérrez demands, "in the light of the Word." That is, we become incapable of recognizing and, a fortiori, of affirming a faith and a theology that are neither rationalistic nor conceptualist but truly incarnational, sacramental in the sense that symbol and referent are intrinsically related. The privileged insight thus comes, not from the perspective of the poor as such, but from the God whom the poor themselves identify as the source of that perspective. The option demanded is not an option for the poor so much as an option for the faith of the poor, an option for the God of the poor.

The lived faith of the poor, specifically popular Catholicism, is precisely a faith lived in the light of the Word which, as such, demands a theological reflection itself illumined by that light. These are a faith and a theology for which historical praxis, context, and experience are always themselves incorporated into a divine praxis: orthopraxis presupposes a theopraxis and, more specifically, a Christopraxis. Thus, the praxis on which theology is based is itself derived from and in-formed by the Word who is received as grace, as gift; it is a praxis incorporated from the outset into a communion of saints which, though mystical and spiritual, is also palpable, visible, and real. In Latino/a popular Catholicism, therefore, the person is in constant, dynamic interaction with the communion of saints, which has the crucified and risen Christ at its center, and which, from the outset, shapes and forms the person's praxis. "God loved us first."

To con-form ourselves to reality is thus, above all, to believe that—and to act as if—"God loved us first," and that love is made concrete historically in the person of the crucified and risen Christ. Faith in Christ, then, is not so much an expression of our search for God as our response to God's search for us. "The people understand the gratuitousness of salvation," writes Diego Irarrazaval; "one can say that popular religion has developed St. Augustine's perspective: faith is a grace. It is not a human product. It is confidence in God." [35]

Whether articulated by sympathizers or by opponents, therefore, any assertion that liberation theology privileges praxis over faith reflects a serious (and dangerous) misreading of the Latin American theological movement, at least as concerns that movement's leading theological figures. Balthasar himself betrays a distorted, superficial reading of praxis-based theologies when he suggests that these fail to distinguish adequately between God's praxis in history and human praxis.[36] As I have attempted to demonstrate above, and continue to argue below, the understanding of Christian faith operative in liberation theologians like Gutiérrez, Sobrino, and Irarrazaval (and in popular Catholicism) is in fact reconcilable with Balthasar's insistence on the priority of God's activity in the world as expressed definitively in the crucified and risen Christ. So, for example, the liberationist interpretations of Christian faith and praxis cited above are quite consistent with the following explanation of the relationship between divine praxis and human praxis, drawn from Balthasar's *Theo-Drama*:

> For what God's primal act in reality was, what implication it had for the world, is . . . something that can only be accepted and pondered in a faith that precedes all personal initiative. . . . Following Christ, which has become possible through his self-surrender, will not consist in doing *some right thing* but in fundamentally surrendering everything, and surrendering it to the God who has totally emptied himself, so that he can use [that right thing] for the world, according to his own purposes.[37]

Conversely, what liberation theology contributes to Balthasar's theological aesthetics is the ability to make more specific and concrete the meaning of "self-surrender." Precisely as historical, such self-surrender necessarily involves a practical solidarity with the crucified and risen Christ as he is visible in the world today, among the crucified people of our own time. For it is precisely they who, like Jesus himself on Calvary, choose daily to "surrender everything to the God who has totally emptied himself," thereby somehow discovering there the strength to go on living and struggling rather than succumbing to despair. Ultimately, their invincible hope makes Hans Urs von Balthasar's God credible.

Like Balthasar, and like Latinos and Latinas, liberation theologians know that the chief threat to the Christian faith today is not atheism but idolatry, not unbelief but what Balthasar has called "rancid religiosity."[38] Liberation theology makes historically concrete the Swiss theologian's own demand that Jesus' humanity be taken seriously. "Why do we take the sacraments (which are human realities) so seriously," asks Balthasar, "while we have so little awareness of the human world of Christ—the human side of his love and his commandment of love, for instance?"[39] Why, indeed! The refusal to take Jesus' humanity seriously, to become saints ourselves, is the greatest scandal, for it undermines the credibility of Christ and the church in the world:

> For the spread of Christianity depends (and always has) on our taking [Christ's commandment of love] absolutely literally, as the sense demands: "I have given you an example, that you also should do as I have done to you. . . . By this all men—all men!—will know that you are my disciples, if you have love for one another." The disciples are never guaranteed that Peter's power of the keys and the institutional side of the Church will convince and convert people. But love can do so; and, wherever it has been taken literally, it always has done so. The saints who genuinely loved even succeeded in making the keys seem appealing and in reconciling those who were distrustful of them, for they are the keys to love and must be used in love. We only have a right to describe the Church as the total sacrament of salvation provided we take the humanity seriously. For the sign-quality—the rite, the matter, the sanctifying word—is essential to the sacrament.[40]

What liberation theologians would add is that, if we are to take Jesus' humanity as seriously as Balthasar demands, the commandment to love can neither remain abstract nor be reduced to individual relationships but must be rooted in a preferential option for the poor, a solidarity with the poor . . . precisely as the means of taking Christ's humanity and his commandment of love absolutely seriously. As Balthasar repeatedly insists, humanity and love are embodied in the figure of a criminal hanging from a cross on Calvary. Consequently, it is *there* where we too must live out the commandment of love, among the innocent victims of our own societies. Our refusal to do so remains the great scandal of Christianity, and the greatest impediment to the credibility of Christ and the church in the world today.

5

Seeing the Form

Theological Aesthetics from the Margins

The lived faith of the poor and, specifically, the everyday encounter with *Cristo Compañero* might be understood as a praxis of, in Hans Urs von Balthasar's phrase, "seeing the Form." "The content . . . ," contends von Balthasar, "does not lie behind the form (*Gestalt*), but within it. Whoever is not capable of seeing and 'reading' the form will, by the same token, fail to perceive the content. Whoever is not illumined by the form will see no light in the content either."[1] U.S. Latino theologian Alejandro García-Rivera explains the act of seeing the form as follows:

"Seeing" the form, like the act of hearing, is not a selective or controlling act, but an act of surrender to that which is "seen." . . . What is being received is the form of that which is other. The reception of that which is other makes unique demands. To receive that which is other means that the other must be received wholly. That which is other can only be experienced in its fullness. Any diminishment of its "otherness," any reduction of detail, any attempt at selectivity is to lose the experience altogether. For it is in the experience of otherness that the inbreaking of God's glory becomes possible. . . . "Seeing" the form, then, amounts to the capacity to receive the whole of a unique difference. That capacity depends on our willingness to be "formed" by the requirements of that which is other. . . . "Seeing" is, paradoxically, an *act* of *receptivity* to that which is other.[2]

In the act of "seeing the form" of revelation, our praxis and reflection become con-formed to that revelation, for what is revealed "is not revelation and precept, but participation, *communio.*"[3]

This is indeed the significance of the encounter between the risen Christ and his disciples. Here, the *communio* that had been sundered when the disciples abandoned Christ on Calvary is reestablished. But it is reestablished not through some sort of interior, spiritual conversion on the part of the disciples; the new *communio* is the result of the utterly unexpected, unanticipated irruption of Christ's scarred body into the upper room. That is to say, what is radically transformative is precisely the objectivity of Christ's appearance (albeit an objectivity that also necessarily includes the subjective dimension of seeing the form of Christ's body, since only those "who have eyes to see" can recognize the body). It is precisely the supremely particular, objective reality of Christ's crucified and risen body that, when perceived and received by the disciples, is capable of engendering a new faith and hope: "The encounter which befalls the witnesses is [Christ's] initiative. It is pure gift—in word and sign, in greeting and blessing, in call, address, instruction, in consolation, command and mission, in the founding of a new community."[4] The sensuous character of the encounter between Jesus and the disciples is, of course, central to the account. However, as Balthasar notes, "It is not on the sensuous experiences that the stress lies. Rather, it is their object which is emphasized, and this latter, the living Christ, shows himself *of his own volition.*"[5] At the same time, Balthasar continues, "The category of mere visionary seeing is not enough; even 'speaking of "objective visions" remains unsatisfactory.' Talk of 'encounter' is here an absolute necessity: encounter, moreover, in which for the first time the quite determinate 'I' of the One encountered is recognized."[6]

Neither a subjectivism that reduces the crucifixion-resurrection to an event interior to the disciples nor an objectivism that reduces it to a merely empirical event can do justice to the reality of the *Cristo Compañero* of the Latino/a community. Our Christ is real, not in spite of the subjective desires and hopes he represents, but precisely because he calls forth from us a subjective response, our own participation in his resurrection. Christ's real presence with us is no mere expression of our own hopes (for which, in far too many cases, there are simply no empirical warrants); rather, our hopes are the subjective response that his gratuitous presence with us calls forth. The possibility of liberation does not generate a symbol that we call "Christ"; rather, the reality of Christ in our midst makes liberation possible and, indeed, enjoins it. Consequently, the wounded, risen body of Christ is intrinsic to what he represents, and vice versa. To sever that body, as symbol, from the liberation that it represents is to obscure precisely what is most radical, transformative, and liberating about the crucifixion-resurrection—namely, its very bodiliness. This is especially true for those historically marginalized peoples whose wounded bodies, like that of Christ, are still today relegated to the other side of the tracks, dangerous memories that must be expunged at all costs.

The unexpected, extravagant nature of God's love in the person of Christ is precisely what makes Christ believable for a people who are themselves scourged, violated, and forgotten. Such a love cannot be anticipated or rationalized in advance; it simply makes no sense in human terms. It can only be received as utterly gratuitous. Juan Diego refused to believe that the Virgin could take any notice of him, much less designate him as her special envoy to the bishop. If theology is to have a role here, notes Balthasar, it will be to "cause the act of God's love for us to appear more divine, more radical, more complete and at the same time more unimaginable and improbable."[7] Every dogma is but the assertion "that God's love extends to this maximum."[8] Liberation theology does precisely this . . . by arguing that the God of the excluded is the one true God, that the Christ of the outcast is indeed the Way, the Truth, and the Life. Incredible!

The kerygma, or content of revelation, is not externally or accidentally related to its particular sociohistorical embodiment in the Word, in the body of Christ. From within, the Word of God itself illumines us, bids us to believe the unbelievable; to perceive the content, we must be able to perceive (receive) its form. "If we allow ourselves to be contemplated by God, and permit God to operate within us," writes Jon Sobrino, "we shall be able to contemplate God and the world in a unified way, and shall be able to love God and the world in a unified way."[9]

The lived faith of the poor thus reflects and retrieves a non-modern (later I suggest "transmodern") understanding of the cosmos as intrinsically symbolic. Latino/a popular Catholicism is a contemporary, concrete example of what Balthasar calls "seeing the Form" insofar as popular Catholic practices presuppose and affirm the real presence of the sacred in our everyday lives. Indeed, Balthasar's project itself represents a magisterial attempt to retrieve the symbolic, or sacramental realism of premodern Christianity. In her own argument for symbolic realism, Latina feminist theologian Michelle Gonzalez quotes von Balthasar:

> The beautiful is above all a *form*, and the light does not fall on this form from above and from outside, rather it breaks forth from the form's interior. . . . Visible form not only "points" to an invisible, unfathomable mystery; form is the apparition of this mystery, and reveals it while, naturally, at the same time protecting and veiling it. . . . The content (*Gehalt*) does not lie behind the form (*Gestalt*), but within it."[10]

Thus, if the great Swiss theologian thus bemoaned contemporary Catholic theology's inability to see the form, U.S. Latino/a theologians are today articulating a theology that, grounded in Latino/a popular Catholicism, suggests that the poor are indeed able—and have always been able—to see the form.

Yet it is precisely the form, I have argued, that is relativized in the modern turn to the subject and deconstructed in the postmodern erasure of the subject. Under the sway of a contemporary, Kantian gnosticism in which form becomes merely a pointer to the content that lies behind the form, we have become increasingly incapable of seeing the form as inseparable from the content of faith. Uncomfortable with the necessarily physical, bodily, and therefore particular character of revelation—in the crucified and risen body of Christ, in the *corpus verum* and *corpus mysticum*, in the *communio sanctorum*—Euro-American and European theologies have too often relativized that body in favor of some presumably more universalizable content that, since it is not intrinsically related to the form, could just as easily be expressed in other forms, could just as easily appear in different clothing. Christ is thus severed from the particular form of his wounded body as it hangs on the cross, appears to the disciples after the resurrection, and is given historically in the Eucharist, the ecclesial community, the church (itself, of course, a social body).

We are uncomfortable, especially, with the wounds on the body of Christ. We sever the wounded body of Christ from the kerygma, which is now free—we assume—to manifest itself in an almost limitless number of forms. Scandalized by the all-too-visible wounds on the *corpus mysticum*, we reject the *corpus verum* in favor of a presumably purer community, a purer faith. The form thus becomes essentially irrelevant, as long as its content is affirmed, a content that is necessarily abstract inasmuch as it exists outside any determinate form; indeed, we often presume that, in order to salvage the content, we must excise it from any particular form. In order to salvage Jesus Christ, we must excise his message, what he represents, from his wounded, concrete, historical body; in order to salvage Christianity, we must excise it (whatever "it" is) from its wounded, concrete, historical body.

The meaning of the kerygma is thus divorced from the wounded historical body in which that kerygma becomes really present in history, even if always also eschatologically. For if God is love, and if God is fully revealed in the person of Jesus Christ, then, as Balthasar avers, "Jesus Christ is what he expresses." Or, in the words of Jon Sobrino, "The genuine Jesus appears both as the bearer of good news and that good news itself."[11] The content of the revelation is accessible in its fullness only in and through the form in which it is expressed. This, indeed, is the scandal of the cross—namely, that "the ideal is only to be found in the real, not behind it."[12] It is, likewise, the scandal of the lived faith of the crucified people. The form of the Christian truth is the cross.

Balthasar unmasks the elitism underlying our inability, as professional theologians, to see the particular form of revelation as a unity of form and content, including the elitism of those of us who desire and claim to be in solidarity with the poor:

> In relation to the central phenomenon of revelation we can by no means speak of "signs" which, according to their nature, point beyond themselves to something "signified." Jesus the Man, in his visibleness, is not a sign pointing beyond himself to an invisible "Christ of faith." . . . Not only everything

sacramental and institutional about the Church, but Christ's whole humanity thus becomes all too clearly something for those "simple" Christians who need material crutches, while the advanced and the perfect can dispense with the symbol, whose spiritual core they have been able to reach.[13]

To suggest that it doesn't ultimately matter what one believes in, what the particular, concrete form of faith's content is, is to fall into a gnosticism that denies the reality of the body and historicity—and it is, conversely, to dismiss as naive or infantile the lived religion of the poor, who refuse to thus "spiritualize" Christian revelation, to spiritualize the body of Christ for fear of its wounds (see chaps. 1 and 2, this volume). To argue that all forms of religious faith are ultimately reducible to some lowest common denominator of core values—and that all that matters is that we abide by these values—is to deny bodily, historical particularity as surely as the assertion of some common humanity on the part of white male Europeans denies the bodily, historical particularity of women and other races and cultures. We cannot have it both ways; we can't insist on the irreducible uniqueness of bodily, historical, particular existence and then deny the irreducible uniqueness of the body of Christ, the body on the cross, in the Eucharist, in the church—and, therefore, the truth claims of that body.

The Western preoccupation with the body as an abstract ideal masks an underlying depreciation of imperfect, scarred, or wounded bodies: the wounded, if glorified, body of Christ as well as the wounded bodies of the crucified people. Gutiérrez notes,

Some Christian milieus, usually in affluent countries, have promoted a reevaluation and "celebration" of the human body in cultural expressions—for example, some modern dances and other bodily forms of expression that are used in eucharistic celebrations. . . . Whatever the merits of this claim, I want to note here that the concern for the corporeal in Latin American spiritual experiences has come about in quite a different way. . . . It is not "*my* body," but the "body of the poor person"—the weak and languishing body of the poor—that has made the material a part of a spiritual outlook.[14]

The failure to see the body of Christ as it is, as a crucified and risen Body, ultimately prevents us from truly appreciating, truly taking seriously the lived faith of the poor, who do not flee from the wounded bodies in their midst to the illusory security of abstract, ideal bodies; they are not concerned with abstract ideals but with real persons, with the real Christ.

The fear that underlies the desire to wipe the wounds from Christ's body thus has manifold manifestations beyond Christology itself. Whether the social body that is the church, or the physical human bodies of the poor, we are repulsed by any body that is wounded—which is to say, we are repulsed by any real body. Referring to the Pauline notion of the body of Christ, Gustavo Gutiérrez observes, "Readers often regard this theology of the church as simply a beautiful metaphor. However, we must, shocking though this idea may be, see through to the realism that characterizes the Pauline approach. He is speaking of the real body of Christ, which he looks upon as an extension of the incarnation."[15] William Cavanaugh observes,

> Many contemporary Christians have shied away from the image of the church as the body of Christ, for naming the church as Christ's very body rings of the ecclesiastical triumphalism of past eras. . . . The danger does not lie, however, in the identification of the church with the body of Christ, but rather in the complete identification of the earthly body with the heavenly. . . . The unfaithfulness of the church in the present age is based to some extent precisely on its failure to take itself seriously as the continuation of Christ's body in the world and to conform itself, body and soul, not to the world but to Christ (Rom. 12:2).[16]

The character of the church as a concrete, historical, social body, a *corpus verum*, has important implications for the Christian theologian. As Gutiérrez insists,

> I begin from the conviction that the theological task is a vocation that arises and is exercised in the heart of the ecclesial community. Indeed, its starting point is the gift of faith in which we welcome the truth of the Word of God,

and its contributions are at the service of the evangelizing mission of the church. This ecclesial location gives theology its raison d'être, determines its scope, nurtures it with the sources of revelation—Scripture and Tradition—enriches it with the recognition of the charism of the magisterium and dialogue with the magisterium, and puts it in contact with other ecclesial functions.[17]

The church's visibility as a distinct social body is a crucial element in its ability to stand in defense of the poor in history; even if not often enough, the visible, institutional church has often been (and certainly in Latin America!) the only viable political counterbalance to military and economic elites.[18] Archbishop Oscar Romero is only the most dramatic example of the prophetic power of the institutional church. (Who else could have dared to demand publicly that the Salvadoran army lay down their arms and be taken seriously—seriously enough to be murdered for saying it?)

"HE HAD NEITHER FORM NOR BEAUTY": TOWARD A LIBERATING THEOLOGICAL AESTHETICS

If the truth of the crucified and risen Christ is a necessary aspect of the liberating character of Christ in the lives of the crucified people, that truth will remain abstract (and thus extrinsic to the figure of Christ) unless it has the power to attract, inspire, and compel; in the words of Balthasar, unless "light breaks forth from the form's interior"[19] and illumines us from within. If the wounded, risen Christ is to be the source of a new, reconciled *communio*, his figure (form) must have the power to draw us to Christ and to his cause. It must have the power to break through all those psychological, emotional, social, and political barriers that would prevent us from seeing the form of a figure that, to most right-minded people and even to the disciples themselves, would initially appear as frightful, if not utterly unbelievable (folly). That power to draw us irresistibly to itself, to inspire and convict, that same power that turned terrified, cowering disciples into a renewed community willing to risk their very lives in order to proclaim the truth they had witnessed, is what—following Balthasar—we might call the aesthetic character of Christian truth.

This aesthetic character is what makes Christian truth inherently sacramental, intrinsically symbolic. Writes David Bentley Hart,

> Beauty's authority, within theology, guards against any tendency toward gnosticism, for two reasons: on the one hand, worldly beauty shows creation to be the real theater of divine glory—good, gracious, lovely, and desirable, participating in God's splendor—and on the other, it shows the world to be unnecessary, an expression of divine glory that is free, framed for God's pleasure, and so neither a defining moment in the consciousness of God nor the consequence of some defect or fall within the divine.[20]

Thus, if the lived faith of the saints, God's holy ones, shows forth the divine glory in a particularly powerful, attractive way, ultimately *all* creation is "the real theater of divine glory." In all its manifestations, the beautiful is the epiphany of God's loving presence in the world and the evidence of that presence. This is what it means to say that creation is intrinsically symbolic, intrinsically sacramental.

If Christ is really present in the world, in our everyday lives, a theological aesthetics safeguards that real presence over against attempts to demythologize, universalize, spiritualize, or internalize Christ: "to demythologize is not to demystify; its ultimate effect is not to ground faith in history or the worldliness of creaturely being, but to de-historicize, to unworld the soul, to make faith the experience of a mystical eschaton in perpetual advent, in the inner core of the present, imparted to the self in its most inviolable subjectivity. The church as a society in time . . . is displaced from the center of faith by the story of the self as a homeless wanderer seeking escape from history."[21] Christ then becomes an object to be admired, at best, or despised, at worst, but he cannot be someone to be followed or accompanied. "The idea of the beautiful," wrote the great demythologizer Rudolf Bultmann, "is of no significance in forming the life of Christian faith, which sees in the beautiful the temptation of a false transfiguration of the world which distracts the gaze from 'beyond.' . . . The beautiful . . . is therefore, as far as the Christian faith is concerned, always something that lies beyond this life."[22] Here, the symbol is reduced to "an afterthought, a speculative appropriation of the aesthetic moment in the service of a supposedly more vital and essential meaning; the symbol is that which arrests the force of the aesthetic, the continuity of the surface, in order to disclose 'depths'; it suspends the aesthetic in favor of the gnoseological, in order to discover something more fundamental than whatever merely 'accidental' form might manifest it."[23] The symbol thus has value only insofar as it can be explained.

The aesthetic character of Christ safeguards the truth and historical reality of the Christian kerygma, and that aesthetic character is nowhere more evident than in the lived faith of the poor. The aesthetic authority of Christ, his power to attract companions (especially from among the poor), makes him credible as a reality; "it is Christ's nearness to the poor that makes him credible," says Sobrino. Conversely, suggests David Bentley Hart, it is precisely that nearness that is folly to the upstanding: "the 'liberal Protestant' project . . . for two centuries sought to abstract from the restive historicality of the *kerygma* some more universally valid content—religious, ethical, social—thus to convey Christ across to a more respectable bank of Lessing's ditch."[24]

In contrast, argues Hart,

The content of Christian faith abounds in particularities, concrete figures, moments like the crucifixion, which cannot simply be dissolved into universal truths of human experience, but stand apart in their historical and aesthetic singularity. To speak of the cross of Christ or even the empty tomb as symbol merely arrests the power of expression—the aesthetic eruption, the linguistic radiance—that each releases, in order to make each explicable in the context of a neutral rationality; it stills the unutterable excess, at once historical and aesthetic, that belongs to both. But the crucifixion and resurrection of Jesus tell us nothing in the abstract about human dereliction or human hope—they are not motifs of a tragic wisdom or goads to an existential resolve—but concern first what happened to Jesus of Nazareth, to whose particular truth and radiance all the general "truths" of human experience must defer. The "symbol," extracted from the complexities of its many contexts, is pure transparency, the paralysis of beauty, yielding before the figureless glare of an abstraction. . . . Theology must always remain at the surface (aesthetic, rhetorical, metaphoric), where all things, finally, come to pass.[25]

The particularity and historicity of Christ's body (the wounds!) are what draw to him all those victims of history whose own historical bodies have for centuries been deemed mere abstractions in the face of progress. His aesthetic power shatters the barriers between the crucified and risen Lord and the millions of crucified victims for whom Christ would otherwise be simply another abstract theological concept incapable of generating hope.

If Christ is able to become really present, it is as *this* beauty, for only this beauty "is oblivious of the boundaries that divide ideal from real, transcendent from immanent, supernatural from natural, pleasing from profound—even, perhaps, nature from grace; 'Crossing these boundaries so forgetfully,' remarks Balthasar, 'belongs to the essence of the beautiful and of aesthetics almost as a necessity.'"[26] Oblivious to the boundaries established by modern notions of symbol, a theological aesthetics can give expression to the reality of Christ as a presence in the lives of the poor, as *Cristo Compañero*.

At the same time, Christ's presence also implies distance: he is not just wounded (as we are) but also risen, not just one of us but also transformative of our painful, sinful reality. *Cristo Compañero* is thus able not only to breach barriers but also to reveal what Hart calls the aesthetic power of difference: "distance is originally the gift of the beautiful—rather than the featureless sublimity of will, or force, or *différence*, or the ontological Nothing. . . ."[27] Because the source of this difference is not conflict or violence (as in Hobbes, or indeed most modern philosophies) but gift, this essential difference between Christ and ourselves is breached not though violence or domination but only through a gratitude that is expressed in worship and in a praxis of solidarity with Christ's activity in the world today. A theological aesthetics rooted in the figure of the crucified and risen Christ thus affirms difference, but does so not in order to assert the inevitability of conflict or power struggles, but, on the contrary, in order to insist on the possibility (and imperative) of a reconciliation that recognizes the beauty of that difference:

> Only thus is it possible to extend analogically the language of God as "Wholly Other" to every other, because the other is seen within and by way of Christ, as the beauty of the infinite, the shape of God's desire and object of his love, the splendor of his glory. Everything Nietzsche deplored about Christianity—its enervating compassion for life at its most debile and deformed, the Gospels' infuriating and debased aesthetic, which finds beauty precisely where a discriminating and noble eye finds only squalor and decadence—is in fact the expression of an order of vision that cannot be confined within the canons of taste prescribed by myths of power and eminence . . . an order of vision . . . which cannot turn away from the other because it has learned to see in the other the beauty of the crucified. Because the God who goes to his death in the form of a slave breaks open hearts, every face becomes an icon: a beauty that is infinite.[28]

The only way of expressing belief in the risen Christ (difference) is through a practical solidarity with the crucified Christ. Indeed, there is no independent field of Christian ethics except as the praxis of con-forming ourselves to the crucified and risen Lord.[29]

Conversely, as I have insisted above, any attempt to impose that belief through the exercise of coercion or violence necessarily contradicts and undermines such belief. (The attempt to impose Christian faith is no more internally coherent than is the attempt to impose a democratic system of government; in both cases, the means are in direct contradiction to the ends—and will be perceived as such by those persons who are the objects of such attempts.) To assert that Christ is the Way, the Truth, and the Life through any type of coercion is impossible without thereby denying in practice what one claims to be asserting in theory. If the truth of Christ is indeed beautiful, it can only attract and compel from inside, through the inherent power of the crucified and risen Christ as he is present today in the world, in Scripture, in the church, and especially in the concrete lives of Christians.

As beautiful, moreover, the difference between Christ and ourselves gives rise to desire, which becomes a necessary aspect of the human response to that difference:

> Here, Christian thought learns something, perhaps, of how the Trinitarian love of God—and the love God requires of creatures—is eros and agape at once: a desire for the other that delights in the distance of otherness. But desire must also be cultivated; the beautiful does not always immediately commend itself to every taste; Christ's beauty, like that of Isaiah's suffering servant, is not expressed in vacuous comeliness or shadowless glamor, but calls for a love that is charitable, that is not dismayed by distance or mystery, and that can repent of its failure to see; this is to acquire what Augustine calls a taste for the beauty of God (*Soliloquia* 1.3-14). . . . And, as Augustine also remarks, it is what one loves—what one desires—that determines to what city one belongs (*Enarrationes in Psalmos* 2.64.2).[30]

Balthasar rejects any easy dichotomy between *agape* ("selfless love of the other as other") and *eros* ("self-centered desire for the other"), suggesting that "it was already obvious to Plato and Plotinus that eros in its highest development was seen as selfless, for it loved the good for the sake of the good."[31] Hence, as so much of the Christian mystical tradition exemplifies, our response to Christ's beauty—precisely qua "beauty"—necessarily involves a desire for union with the Beloved, a desire that is itself prompted by God's own desire for us, as revealed above all on the cross. It is no coincidence that the greatest mystical poetry is also romantic poetry—for example, the Song of Songs, the poems of St. John of the Cross.

Latina feminist theologians have also insisted that desire is a necessary aspect of a lived, and therefore embodied, Christian faith—and, in the Latino/a community, that desire is expressed, above all, in popular religious practices.[32] Yet the desire elicited by the crucified and risen Christ is a response linked inextricably to the praxis of justice. The particularity and historicity of the beautiful, as made present in this figure, precludes any notion of beauty that ignores the wounds, the dangerous memories forever inscribed on Christ's risen body. Just as the life vindicated by the resurrection is no life in general, but life in solidarity with the crucified victims of history, so too is the desire evoked by this aesthetic symbol not a passion for life in general, but an affirmation of the possibility of reconciliation. In the person of the crucified and risen Christ, the human desire for the beautiful is revealed as but a response to God's own prior, passionate desire for us, a desire that—as the apostle Thomas discovered—will not be forever frustrated.

A Christian theology of beauty, or theological aesthetics, can only be grounded in the particularity of the crucified and risen Christ and in our practical response to him, in our solidarity with him as we encounter him today among the crucified victims of our societies. The appropriate response to the beauty of the crucified and risen Christ can only be the act of solidarity, the praxis of accompaniment that includes the imperative of "taking the victim down from the cross."[33] In that response alone is revealed the radical difference between a merely human aesthetics and a Christian, divine aesthetics in which the paradigmatic form of God's glory is that of a criminal hanging from a cross. Our response of solidarity with the criminals of history is what transforms an aesthetic theology, where beauty remains an abstraction divorced from the particularity of the crucified and risen Christ, into a theological aesthetics that makes demands on us. It is the difference between the beauty of Mount Tabor, which so enthralled the apostles that they did not want to leave, and the subversive beauty of Calvary, which they sought to avoid at all costs—even though Jesus himself had commanded them to leave Tabor and follow him to Calvary. The starting point for a Christian theological aesthetics is the One who "had no form or beauty":

> He had no form or comeliness that we should look
> at him, and no beauty that we should desire him.
> He was despised and rejected by all;
> *a man of sorrows,* and acquainted with grief;
> and as one from whom people hide their faces
> he was despised, and we esteemed him not.

> Surely he has borne our griefs and carried our
>   sorrows;
> yet we esteemed him stricken, smitten by God,
>   and afflicted.
> But he was wounded for our transgressions,
> he was bruised for our iniquities;
> upon him was the chastisement that made us whole,
> and with his stripes we are healed.
> All we like sheep have gone astray
> we have turned every one to his own way;
> and *the Lord has laid on him the iniquity of us all.*
>   (Isa. 53:2-6; RSV)

It is in our response to the one despised and rejected that he is revealed as truly the form of divine beauty. It is in our response of solidarity that the one "stricken, smitten by God, and afflicted" is revealed as truly the chosen one of God.

What prevents a theological aesthetics from degenerating into a narcissistic aestheticism is precisely the particular, concrete content of this religious symbol, the crucified and risen Christ. Without that particularity, the desire elicited by beauty would be incapable of making the distinctions intrinsic to the praxis of justice, and therefore of truly affirming difference. Ironically—given the post-modernists' rejection of universals—the postmodern affirmation of difference in general is really not an affirmation of difference at all. If all is difference, then all is the same:

> It is not simply difference as such upon which God bestows his approbation, but the content of what differs, the particularity of each thing, the creature's place in the analogical discourse that creation is. Dionysus is a god who cavorts among corpses, and thus affirms all things; the God who creates for his delight and out of love pursues his lost even into the depths of hell, and thus affirms all things. . . . Dionysus cannot be concerned—in the midst of being's wanton and extravagant play—with lost sheep. . . . But for Christian thought it is God's transcendence that alone allows differences to differ, that permits a common thematic medium

between different series, that gives them their ability to elaborate upon and embellish one another, and that looks upon, loves, and elects what differs.[34]

What alone makes possible an affirmation of all life, of all human persons, of all creation, is an affirmation of this particular life, which, having been abandoned to the agony of the cross, has now been resurrected and reconciled. Having affirmed the beauty of life on Calvary, where Christ's love endures even in the face of abandonment, one can go on to affirm the beauty of life in general (or life on Mount Tabor); the reverse is not the case. Our solidarity with the victims of history is the criterion of our love of life, for "it is not the beauty of the cross, but of *the one crucified*, that is rescued at Easter."[35] And the source of that solidarity, the crucified and risen victim, empowers us to draw distinctions between victim and oppressor, life and death, Calvary and Tabor. Far from implying the eradication of difference, Christ is the common ground of all difference, the one who makes difference possible.

The difference that Christ embodies is always in relation to the reconciliation that is its ground and end; the abandonment of Calvary is experienced as painful precisely in relation to another reality, the reality of a reconciled existence. The wounds appear on Christ's resurrected body. Without their context, the wounds would themselves be experienced as fundamental reality, as "all there is."[36] As John Paul II writes, the cross reveals its power (for both destruction and redemption) only in the context of the resurrection:

> For through faith the Cross reaches man *together with the Resurrection*: the mystery of the Passion is contained in the Paschal Mystery. The witnesses of Christ's Passion are at the same time witnesses of his Resurrection. Paul writes: "That I may know him (Christ) and the power of his Resurrection, and may share his sufferings, becoming like him in his death, that if possible I may attain the resurrection from the dead." Truly, the Apostle first experienced the "power of the Resurrection" of Christ, on the road to Damascus, and only later, in this paschal light, reached that "sharing in his sufferings" of which he speaks, for example, in the Letter to

the Galatians. *The path of Paul* is clearly paschal: *sharing in the Cross* of Christ comes about *through the experience of the Risen One,* therefore through a special sharing in the Resurrection. Thus, even in the Apostle's expressions on the subject of suffering there so often appears the motif of glory, which finds its beginning in Christ's Cross.[37]

This is why, paradoxically, those who most profoundly experience God's absence, who experience themselves abandoned, are also so often the ones who most profoundly experience God's presence. It is in relationship to God's nearness that we experience God's distance (since "distance" and "absence" are, by definition, relative terms). Indeed, as Simone Weil observes, the agonizing experience of God's absence is itself a form of presence: "Two prisoners whose cells adjoin communicate with each other by knocking on the wall. The wall is the thing which separates them but is also their means of communication. It is the same with us and God. Every separation is a link."[38]

It makes perfect sense, then, that the holy person, the person closest to God, is the one who most intensely experiences his or her distance from God. Those who most intimately know God's presence are also those who most profoundly experience God's absence. It is at the moment that Thomas sees Jesus' wounds and is invited to touch them—the moment of conversion—that Thomas simultaneously experiences most intensely the anguish of his, and the other apostles', own sinful distance from God. Thus, our experience of God's distance or silence presupposes a more fundamental experience of God's presence. It is when he witnesses and hears Christ's cry of abandonment on the cross that the Roman centurion realizes that he has seen the form of God's own love: "Truly, this was God's Son!"

6

Reimagining the Border

Liberation Theological Aesthetics and Globalization

A theological aesthetics grounded in U.S. Latino/a popular Catholicism reflects the intrinsic connection between worship, social justice, and theological truth. In so doing, such a theological aesthetics makes sociohistorically concrete Balthasar's theological aesthetics, thereby precluding its degeneration into a neoconservative, sacramental triumphalism inattentive to its sociopolitical context and implications. At the same time, a Latino/a Catholic theological aesthetics makes theologically concrete the preferential option for the poor, thereby precluding its degeneration into a liberal social activism inattentive to its rationalist and instrumentalist presuppositions (which simply reinforce rather than resist consumerist Western cultures). In this chapter, I suggest, more specifically, that the history of Latino/a communities as borderland communities makes historically concrete the symbol of the crucified and risen Christ in a way that precludes its usurpation for either neoconservative or liberal purposes.

As indicated above, Balthasar chastises contemporary theologies for failing to "take the humanity of Christ seriously." Shouldn't Catholics, he asks, take Jesus' humanity and, specifically, his commandment of love as literally as they take the sacraments? We ought to view the symbol of Jesus Christ through the same lens we view the sacraments—namely, one that presumes the intrinsic unity of symbol and symbolized; if the Eucharist, for instance, is what it symbolizes, so too is that foundational sacrament of God, Jesus Christ himself. And to take the humanity of Jesus seriously means to take seriously the fact that Jesus did not only become human; he became a particular human person in a particular time and place—and continues to be revealed in particular persons in particular times and places. Balthasar wonders out loud why "we have so little awareness of the human world of Christ—the human side of his love and his commandment of love."

With its strong emphasis on Jesus' humanity, Latino/a popular Catholicism can make an important contribution to a Catholic theological aesthetics that "takes the humanity of Christ seriously." More specifically, the lived faith of Latino/a Catholics brings to bear a social perspective missing—or at least underplayed—in Balthasar's theological aesthetics, a lacuna that undermines the Swiss theologian's own attempt to take Jesus' humanity seriously. The particularity of Christ's humanity is precisely what makes the Gospel good news to the poor. The specificity of his humanity prevents the symbol of Christ, as the sacrament of God, from becoming decontextualized, spiritualized, and thus reduced to a mere abstraction incapable of generating resistance in the world and infinitely manipulable in the service of political power and economic gain (whether by multinational corporations, the state, or religious leaders). That is, without greater attention to the particular humanity of Christ, Balthasar's own theological aesthetics remains susceptible to a neo-gnostic spiritualization. Once again, I would suggest that, rather than conflict with Balthasar's project, the preferential option for the poor as developed by liberation theologians and U.S. Latino and Latina theologians can complement and contribute to his theological aesthetics.

The work of U.S. Latino and Latina theologians has drawn attention to the humanity of Christ while suggesting that Euro-American notions of Christ's humanity do not take seriously the specific contours of that humanity. Mexican American theologian Virgilio Elizondo focuses in a special way on the theological significance of Jesus' social location in Galilee; Jesus of Nazareth was a Jew from Galilee. Consequently, argues Elizondo, any Christology that claims to be rooted in the Gospels—and that takes seriously the Christian doctrine of the incarnation—must take as its starting point the historical-theological particularity of Jesus Christ. That particularity, including his distinctiveness as a Jew from Galilee, is not merely accidental to the Christian kerygma; it is at the very heart of the kerygma. Likewise, a theological aesthetics that takes as its starting point the crucified and risen Christ must be attentive to the glory of God as revealed definitively in the One "who had no beauty or form"; God's glory is made manifest in Christ's identity not only as a Jew, not only as a carpenter's son, but as a Jewish carpenter's son who was from Galilee. That social location forced a revalorization or inversion of his society's presuppositions of what constitutes beauty, was perceived as threatening and subversive, and eventually led to his crucifixion. Christ's particularity thus specifies the inherently subversive character of a Christian theological aesthetics.

If Balthasar insists on taking seriously Jesus' historical particularity, he does not explicitly outline the implications of such an insistence; Latin American liberation theologians and U.S. Latino and Latina theologians do. Moreover, these implications are spelled out without denying—or so I would submit—the fundamental insights of Balthasar with respect to the priority of God's praxis in the world and the sacramental, or symbolic realism inherent in Balthasar's notion of theo-drama. Indeed, an increased attention to Jesus' social location would contribute to a theological aesthetics precisely by further specifying the historical particularity, or form of God's glory as the starting point of a Christian theological aesthetics. Jesus was a Jew identified, not with the center of religio-political power in Jerusalem, but with the border region of Galilee; this fact was not incidental to his identity as the crucified and risen Lord, but was a key contributing factor in his condemnation and crucifixion. The theological-ethical significance of Galilee as a borderland brings to light ethical ramifications of a theological aesthetics beyond those that Balthasar himself adumbrates. Again, Balthasar repeatedly warns against aesthetic theologies, yet, because of his resistance to liberation and other praxis-based theologies, his project remains susceptible to an interpretation that, in his own words, does not take seriously the humanity of Christ and the commandment of love.

CHRIST ON THE BORDER

What does Galilee, then, contribute to our understanding of Jesus Christ? I have already suggested how the figure of the crucified and risen Christ, especially as present in Latino/a popular Catholicism and Latin American liberation theologies, can ground a Christian theological aesthetics sociopolitically in the historical experience of the crucified peoples of our societies. Now I want to suggest that Jesus' identity not with the geographical center of Jerusalem but with the hinterland of Galilee can ground a theological aesthetics in the experience of those very marginalized peoples who today represent the most vital segment of the Christian world.

Beyond the Christ of the kings and princes, beyond the Christ of the theologians and philosophers, beyond the Christ of the clerics and bishops, is the Christ of Juan Diego. This Christ is found in a borderland region far from the thrones of power and influence, literally on the margins of society. The border is thus a central concept for understanding the historical particularity of Jesus Christ; in a very special way, the border defined him and his mission. The Galilean borderland frames Jesus' life, death, and resurrection; it is from whence he comes and where he is going. Consequently, we cannot take seriously Jesus' humanity without taking seriously the place of Galilee in his life and mission. This is where the glory of God is revealed, not only in the terrifying silence of Calvary and the shocking vision of the risen Christ, but in the Jewish peoples of the Galilean borderland, that godforsaken place from which nothing good had ever come.

If indeed the borderland is not merely a geographical but, more profoundly, a theological category, a place that makes present the glory of God, how might the God of Jesus Christ be encountered on the border? At the same time, however, we must ask how the dominant U.S. culture's understanding of that border and the U.S. Hispanic understanding of the border may influence our reading of the border as a *locus theologicus*. Thus, before examining the reality of a Christ on the border, we must consider how such a Christ presupposes and demands a transvaluation of the border as interpreted by the dominant culture.

THE FRONTIER

> . . . I am become a name
> For always roaming with an hungry heart,

Much have I seen and known . . .
I am a part of all that I have met;
Yet all experience is an arch, where thro'
Gleams that untravelled world, whose margin fades
Forever and forever when I move.
How dull it is to pause, to make an end.
To rust unburnished, not to shine in use!
And this gray spirit yearning in desire
To follow knowledge like a shining star
Beyond the utmost bound of human thought.
. . . Come my friends,
'Tis not too late to seek a newer world.
Push off, and sitting well in order smite
The sounding furrows; for my purpose holds
To sail beyond the sunset, and the baths
Of all the Western stars until I die
To strive, to seek, to find and not to yield.[1]

With those words from Tennyson's "Ulysses," American historian Frederick Jackson Turner ended his commencement address at the University of Washington in June 1914. Tennyson's words evoked for Turner those frontier ideals that had served the United States so well until the end of the nineteenth century: "to seek a newer world . . . to sail beyond the sunset . . . to strive, to seek, to find and not to yield."

Indeed, it does not take much imagination to see reflected in these words not only the spirit of Daniel Boone and Andrew Jackson but also the spirit of Christopher Columbus and Hernán Cortés. The frontier is the foundational myth of modernity; it is our creation myth. The modern world is constructed by forging and conquering new frontiers: "The first ideal of the pioneer was that of conquest."[2]

In what has been called "the most influential piece of writing in the history of American history," his 1893 essay on "The Significance of the Frontier in American History," Frederick Jackson Turner set forth what came to be known as the frontier thesis:

American social development has been continually beginning over again on the frontier. This perennial rebirth, this fluidity of American life, this expansion westward with its new opportunities, its continuous touch with the simplicity of primitive society, furnish the forces dominating American character. In this advance, the frontier is the outer edge of the wave—the meeting point between savagery and civilization. . . . And now, four centuries from the discovery of America, at the end of a hundred years of life under the Constitution, the frontier has gone.[3]

By the end of the nineteenth century, the western frontier "finally closed forever, with uncertain consequences for the American future."[4]

Yet myths do not easily die when historical conditions change; they may simply be adapted to the new context. Indeed, argued Turner, the values and worldview implicit in the frontier myth have become a part of U.S. culture: "Long after the frontier period of a particular region of the United States has passed away, the conception of society, the ideals and aspirations which it produced, persist in the minds of the people. . . . This experience has been wrought into the very warp and woof of American thought."[5] And Turner's very definition of the frontier myth (as quoted above) already suggests the particular conception of society underlying the myth. Herein lies the fundamental characteristic of the frontier myth, which gives it its power and rationale; the frontier is "the meeting point between savagery and civilization."

In the history and culture of the United States, the very drive to extend the frontier came to be seen as a constitutive feature of civilization itself: to be civilized *is* to extend the frontier, to expand, to seek new opportunities, to dominate, to conquer (in Tennyson's words, "How dull it is to pause, to make an end"). Conversely, then, to accept limits to this expansion is to undermine the very foundations of civilized society: "once free lands were exhausted . . . the whole moral fabric would collapse and the land descend into the state of depravity and tyranny that overcrowded Europe already knew."[6] Thus, implicit in the frontier myth is the assumption that the only alternatives to expansion are decline or degeneration. This raises the question that Turner and other scholars were asking at the turn of the twentieth century: How will the United States react to the closing of the western frontier? Turner did not live to see the emergence of an answer during the remaining decades of the twentieth century.

In the first years of the twenty-first century, however, I do think we can suggest an answer, an answer that lies not to the west but to the south. In retrospect, the turn of the twentieth century represented not so much the demise of the frontier as the replacement of the western frontier with a southern frontier. The westward territorial expansion, including the annexation of Mexican territory in the first half of the nineteenth century, was replaced by a southern expansion. Initially, this latter movement followed the pattern of military, geographical, and political expansion. Thus, in the first half of the twentieth century, the U.S. frontier became the Caribbean and Central America. Just as the western frontier had expanded into virgin territory, so, too, would the southern frontier. After all, there is only one America, only one America the Beautiful. "America" *is* the United States, and the United States would expand its control into its own backyard, particularly the Caribbean and Central America.

Thus, a new breed of pioneers rose up in the first decades of the twentieth century, not only individual adventurers, but also economic enterprises seeking to expand their markets, often in conjunction with U.S. political interests. The rapid growth of multinational corporations during this period provided possibilities for economic expansion unknown to earlier pioneers. When territorial expansion proved impracticable, more benign forms of economic expansion would take its place, even if sometimes with the aid of political and even military intervention and occupation. By the 1930s, contends historian Walter LaFeber, overt military intervention "had become too costly. Nor were such blatantly imperialist gestures any longer needed. The blunt instruments were replaced with the Good Neighbor's economic leverage."[7] Nevertheless, when the economic leverage weakened—for example, between the Eisenhower and Reagan presidencies—U.S. interests might require renewed political and military fortification.

Already in 1890, U.S. Secretary of State James G. Blaine had foreseen the form that the new frontier would take: "he pointedly observed, 'Our great demand is expansion,' but only in trade, for 'we are not seeking annexation of territory.'"[8] Between 1898 and 1901, the United States began to export capital to a degree previously unequalled and, by World War I, had erased its trade deficits.[9] As LaFeber has argued, "The dynamic new United States necessarily prepared itself to find fresh frontiers abroad to replace the closed frontier at home."[10] Moreover, U.S. activity on these fresh frontiers to the south would bear the marks of the earlier westward expansion, drawing on the same historical myth. U.S. attempts to extend its southern frontier "rested on views of history, the character of foreign peoples [i.e., 'savagery'], and politics that anticipated attitudes held by North Americans throughout much of the twentieth century. . . . North Americans seldom doubted that they could teach people to the south to act more civilized."[11] Old attitudes dies hard.

If, as Frederick Jackson Turner averred, the frontier myth has been "wrought into the very warp and woof of American thought," the end of the nineteenth century did not signal the end of the frontier myth, only its relocation and reconceptualization. The persistence of that myth raises important questions for our society more than a century later. The United States is once again confronted with questions concerning the relationship between national identity and geographical boundaries. If the United States of the 1890s perceived national identity as linked to the western frontier, and thus feared a future with closed frontiers, contemporary political, military, and legislative attacks against illegal aliens suggest that the United States today perceives national identity as linked, not to the frontier, but to the border, and fears a future with open borders.

If Turner's suggestion concerning the foundational character of the frontier myth is accurate, we should not assume that, simply because we now prefer the language of borders to the language of frontiers, the difference in terminology reflects a truly different understanding of history and identity. It may be that today the frontier myth still functions as the lens through which we as a society read the reality of our borders, especially the southern border which, in the first decades of this century, became our new, fresh frontier.

FROM A FRONTIER CHRISTIANITY
TO A BORDERLAND CHRISTIANITY

The frontier myth was not, however, unique to the United States. Its roots in modernity informed not only the English colonies of the North but, as Enrique Dussel and others have argued, drove the Spanish and Portuguese conquest/evangelization of the South. For five centuries, the Catholic Church viewed the peoples of Latin America as objects of evangelization: "At best, the Spaniards considered the Indians coarse, childlike, immature . . . , needy of patient evangelization."[12] Thus, through its role in the conquest of the New World, the church itself participated in the drive to extend the western frontier of Western (Christian) civilization: "Cortés carried a banner of black taffeta with a colored cross, and blue and white flames scattered throughout. He inscribed on the border of the banner: *We follow the cross and in this sign we shall conquer.*"[13] The military conquest was thus accompanied by a "spiritual conquest."[14]

Christianity also accompanied and legitimated the establishment of the English colonies in the North: "The Puritans who came to New England frequently drew analogies between their experience and that of ancient Israel . . . for they were in the process of creating a new nation in a new wilderness."[15] By definition, such a wilderness was not inhabited by full-fledged human beings: "Indians were conveniently perceived not so much as ordinary human beings but as part of the fauna, along with buffaloes and coyotes, to be driven off or killed."[16] Thus, in 1645, Roger Williams was able to write: "These *Heathen* Dogges, better kill a thousand of them than that we *Christians* should be endangered or troubled with them; Better they were all cut off, and then we shall have no more trouble with them. . . . Cut them all off, and so make way for Christians."[17] Forrest Wood notes, moreover, the intrinsic connection between political and religious language: "Barbarian, savage, heathen, pagan. Whatever term was used, it designated an incarnation of the source of all evil—Satan. . . . And early American Protestants saw him connected to Africans and Indians."[18] Hence, there was a similar connection between political ("colonization," "civilization") and religious ("evangelization") imperialism:

> It does not require a particularly careful examination to discover that, underneath all of the political shibboleths and economic realizations, Manifest Destiny was, in the final analysis, a *religious* concept that was exalted by Americans of all social levels and had been an essential element in the adventures of every European colonial power. . . . By the sixteenth century, the Reformation itself had become "the grand means employed by God in preparing a people who should lay the foundation of a Christian empire in the New World."[19]

The nature of that Christian empire was specified precisely: "In claiming a divine mandate, Americans did not consign responsibility to some vague universal *élan vital* like 'Providence' or 'Nature,' or, for that matter, even something so general as a biblical God. The Christian imperialist was nothing if not specific. From the first colonial settlement to the late twentieth century, Christian America meant *Protestant* America."[20]

Thus, if Catholic Christianity had been instrumental in the conquest of the South, Protestant Christianity was a dominant (though by no means the only) force in the conquest of the North. They both shared a belief, legitimated by their theologies, that they had been divinely mandated to extend the frontier of Christian civilization into the New World. On the other side of that frontier lay the ever-present threat of contamination and impurity.

Yet, from the beginning, Christian support for imperialism was not monolithic. Among the Spaniards, Bartolomé de Las Casas was only the most famous of a small but significant number of prophetic voices decrying the conquest.[21] Among British colonists, a few Protestant ministers such as Jeremiah Evarts challenged British expansionism.[22] At great personal cost, prophets arose to challenge the churches' all-too-easy appropriation of the frontier myth as the lens through which they would view their evangelizing mission; authentic evangelization, as Las Casas observed, is utterly incompatible with conquest and destruction. Indeed, it is the very opposite.

THE BORDER

Despite the similarities between the northern and southern expansions, significant differences later informed the understanding of the border in North and South. The Latin American perception of the border is rooted in the distinctive history of Latin America itself. As I suggested in chapter 1, while the modern drive for territorial expansion and domination is at the heart of both the Iberian and British colonization of the Americas, the processes of expansion developed differently in the North and South.[23] Justo González argues that this historical difference has given rise to different conceptions of the border:

> Because the Spanish colonizers were forced to live with the original inhabitants of the land, a *mestizo* population and culture developed. . . . In contrast, in the lands to the north, the process and the myth were of a constantly moving frontier, pushing back the native inhabitants of the land, interacting with them as little as possible. There was civilization this side of the frontier; and a void at the other side. The West was to be "won." The western line, the frontier, was seen as the growing edge; but it was expected to produce growth by mere expansion rather than by interaction.[24]

In the North, the border is perceived as moving in only one direction, outward; in the South, the border is perceived as allowing for movement in both directions. In the North, any movement back across the border is thus perceived as "an incursion of the forces of evil and backwardness into the realm of light and progress."[25]

Yet a border need not function as a frontier that only expands and excludes; it need not be perceived as the boundary that protects civilization from savagery. Even if too often denied in practice, an alternative understanding of the border is implicit in the mestizo history of Latin America:

A border is the place at which two realities, two worldviews, two cultures, meet and interact. . . . At the border growth takes place by encounter, by mutual enrichment. A true border, a true place of encounter, is by nature permeable. It is not like medieval armor, but rather like skin. Our skin does set a limit to where our body begins and where it ends. Our skin also sets certain limits to our give-and-take with our environment, keeping out certain germs, helping us to select that in our environment which we are ready to absorb. But if we ever close up our skin, we die.[26]

A border may function to affirm differences while allowing for an interaction that will be mutually enriching. If the drive to conquer others and expand the border outward has legitimated rape and murder, the mestizo children of that violent encounter are living witnesses to a hope and life that are born even in the midst of despair and death. The border is not only a cemetery but a seedbed; not only a Calvary but a manger. The mestizo history of Latin America is evidence that ambiguity can be the seedbed of new life, the border can be the birthplace of a new human community. Such a recognition of the ambiguity of all human histories is a necessary precondition for an understanding of the difference between a frontier and a border.[27] It is a precondition for understanding the difference between "America" and the United States, between an "American" and an "*estadounidense.*"[28]

GOD CHOOSES WHAT THE WORLD REJECTS

Recognition of the ambiguity of human history is also a precondition for encountering the Christ of the Gospels, who is revealed, above all, on the border. It is no mere coincidence that, in the Synoptic accounts, Jesus comes from Nazareth, in Galilee; meets his end in Jerusalem; and, finally, returns to Galilee, where he appears to the apostles after his resurrection (Mark 14:28; Matt 26:32; 28:7, 10, 16).

That Galilee is at the very center of God's self-revelation in Jesus Christ is no mere accident of history. Contiguous with non-Jewish territories and geographically distant from Jerusalem, Galilee was often viewed by first-century Jews as "a Jewish enclave in the midst of 'unfriendly' gentile seas."[29] "The area as a whole, " writes Richard Horsley, "was a frontier between the great empires in their historical struggles."[30]

The Jewish traditions of Galilean peasants were different from those practiced in Jerusalem:

> Galilee was heir in some form to the traditions of the North- ern Kingdom. . . . Torah was important, as was circumcision in Galilean society, but not the written and oral Torah as interpreted by the Judean and Jerusalem retainer class and enforced where they could by the Temple aristocracy. Rather Galilee was home to popular legal and wisdom traditions. . . . Galilee was also ambivalent about Jerusalem, the Temple, the priestly aristocracy, temple dues and tithes.[31]

In short, as Richard Horsley argues, Galilean Jewish practices could be described as a kind of popular religion:

> The distinction anthropologists often make between the "great tradition" and the "little traditions" may be of some help in formulating the issues. A "society" may develop cultural traditions at two levels: the traditions of origin and customary practice continue as a popular tradition cultivated orally in the villages, while specialists codify those same traditions in a standardized and centralized form as an official tradition, which is cultivated orally but perhaps also reduced to written form. Something like this distinction between official tradition and popular tradition may help explain the situation in Galilee as seen both in sources from the first century C.E. and in early rabbinic literature.[32]

The history of Galilee as a land under contention and a political crossroads resulted in the emergence of popular religious practices which reflected that history:

> The bulk of the Galilean population, . . . while not Judean, would likely have been other descendants of former Israelites. While sharing certain common Israelite traditions with the

Judeans, they would have had traditions of their own and distinctive versions of the shared Israelite traditions. Yet it is also inherently unlikely that all Galileans in late second-temple times were descendants of former Israelites. . . . Thus at least some of those living in Galilee must have been non-Israelites, ethnically or in cultural heritage. . . . Within the same village, Israelites and Gentiles lived in adjacent houses or shared the same courtyard . . . , or perhaps even shared a house or oven. . . . A great variety of cooperation between Israelite and Gentile peasants took place on a regular basis.[33]

In the Gospels, the Galilean reality takes on soteriological significance as the place that defines the very character of the Christian revelation, for the good news is incarnated in the person of Jesus Christ. "Galilee did indeed function," observes Sean Freyne, "as a symbol of the newness of Jesus' vision in contrast to the more established circles of Jewish belief for the early Christians, but all the indications are that the symbolic reference was grounded in an actual ministry that was conducted in the real Galilee of the first century CE."[34] This "newness" characterizes Galilee; this is the newness of the borderland—of all borderlands—as, quite literally, marginal to the centers of power.[35]

The crucified and risen Christ is a Jew from the borderland; his ministry and mission, especially, begin and end in the borderland. Like so many human societies throughout history, the ruling elites in Jesus' world attached a moral and indeed theological value to the borderlands. The Jewish establishment in Jerusalem could not conceive that God's word could be revealed among the people of the borderland: "Search and you will see that no prophet is to rise from Galilee" (John 7:52).

Moreover, it is precisely in the midst of the Jewish population of the borderland that the resurrected Christ, the now-glorified Witness to God's power and love, would be encountered: "he has risen from the dead, and behold, he is going before you to Galilee; there you will see him" (Matt. 28:7). Just as the ministry and mission that define Jesus Christ as Son of God had begun in Galilee, so would that ministry and mission find their eschatological fulfillment in Galilee: "there you will see him." Jesus' ministry would end where it began; in Galilee his disciples would see the resurrected Jesus. The culture of the borderland is the privileged locus of God's self-revelation. God becomes incarnate in a Galilean Jew, who is crucified in Jerusalem, is raised from the dead, and, now in glorified form, returns to the Galilean borderland, where his disciples are gathered and the new *ekklesia* is born. In the Gospels, this borderland reality takes on theological significance as the place that defines the very character of the Christian revelation, for the good news is incarnated in the person of Jesus Christ, Jesus the Jew from the borderland. Jesus Christ's social location is not merely accidental to the Christian kerygma; it is at the very heart of our Christian faith. The borderland thus takes on explicitly theological, soteriological import as a specification of the epistemological privilege of the poor: insofar as the border functions to exclude, those persons who are excluded are in a privileged position to recognize the crucified and risen Christ, who himself was and continues to be excluded.

In making this point, however, I want to insist on the inescapable significance of the borderland as a privileged *locus theologicus* while acknowledging the dangers of too-simplistic interpretations of Jesus' identity as a Jew from Galilee. That is, my concern is to discern the ongoing, historical, theological relevance of Galilee. Such a concern is, of course, itself related to the historical Jesus and the historical Galilee, but the latter (which is as hotly debated among contemporary scholars as has been the historical Jesus) cannot foreclose the continuing theological role of Galilee any more than the former has foreclosed christological investigation. The Scriptures are not merely a historical text but a living text, which includes the ongoing practices of the faith community in which that text is given life; the practices themselves become part of the text that must be interpreted theologically. My claim has been that U.S. Latino/a popular Catholicism represents precisely such a collection of religious practices.

In this regard, I agree with Michael Lee's perceptive interpretation of Virgilio Elizondo's treatment of the Galilean Jesus. While acknowledging the appropriateness and, indeed, necessity of several recent critiques of that treatment, Lee argues that Elizondo's fundamental concern remains *pastoral* (while historical accuracy is essential, it is not sufficient and not an end in itself):

In *Galilean Journey* Elizondo does not seek to describe the historical Jesus, but rather focuses on the theological import for the reader of the Gospels' portrayal of Jesus as a Galilean. Elizondo reminds us that Galilee, as it is theologically and symbolically evoked in the Gospels, represents a marginality that resonates with the marginal location of U.S. Latino/as who read the Gospels today. . . . While John Meier describes Jesus as a "marginal Jew in a marginal province at the eastern end of the Roman empire," Elizondo offers insight into the significance of that marginality from the margin itself.[36]

Thus, when I suggest that U.S. Latino/a popular Catholicism provides historical particularity to christological claims, I am suggesting that the lived faith of U.S. Hispanics—rooted in but not limited to the historical Jesus—reveals important aspects of the crucified and risen Christ as he is present in Scripture *and* in the ongoing life of the faith community.

Such a distinction is important as a safeguard against the interpretive dangers discussed by Lee and articulated by contemporary scholars such as Jean-Pierre Ruiz and Jeffrey Siker—most important being the danger of a latent anti-Judaism.[37] As Lee points out, what makes Galilee a theologically privileged locus is its identification with the margins, the borderland, with exclusion and rejection—and, therefore, with contemporary loci of exclusion and rejection. What makes the borderland a locus of prophetic resistance is precisely the claim that those who have been excluded do indeed belong in the community as full participants. In other words, the prophetic character of Galilee presupposes an unambiguous affirmation of Jesus' identity as a Jew; if he had not been a Jew, he would have had no claims on Jerusalem. Likewise, as people of the borderlands, U.S. Latinos/as stand in a prophetic relationship to the United States precisely insofar as Hispanics claim to belong to a community that does not accept them as full participants. Lacking such a claim, there can be no prophetic critique. The established authorities reject those precise claims: Jesus' claim to be a full-fledged Jew, Hispanics' claim to be full-fledged Americans. The claim that popular Catholicism belongs to *the* Catholic tradition gives the former its prophetic character.

EVANGELIZING THE EVANGELIZERS

Many centuries after Christ—on another border, that between Europe and America, between North and South—the church of the Americas was itself born in the borderland, in the encounter between *la Virgen morena* (the dark-skinned virgin), or Our Lady of Guadalupe, and a poor indigenous man, Juan Diego. The appearance of Our Lady of Guadalupe in December 1531 signals a turning point or axial point in the history of Christianity in the Americas; at the very heart of Mexican history stands the figure of Our Lady of Guadalupe. Here, another resurrection took place, the resurrection of the Mexican people out of the ashes of conquest—once again, a resurrection on the border. Among those ashes, the Virgin of Guadalupe and Juan Diego dare to proclaim the good news to a people who had been decimated by their Spanish Christian conquerors. In so doing, Guadalupe and Juan Diego reveal themselves as the true evangelizers of the Americas.

The popular devotion to Our Lady of Guadalupe is based on the *Nican Mopohua*, a text dating from the 1560s and written in Náhuatl, the language of the indigenous Nahua people. The events recounted took place in 1531, not long after the Nahua defeat at the hands of the invading Spanish *conquistadores*, "ten years after the conquest of Mexico City."[38] In the Guadalupe event, *la Virgen morena* appears to Juan Diego on a hill outside what is now Mexico City. The narrative recounts several encounters between *La Morenita* and Juan Diego, in the course of which she repeatedly assures him that, despite his own sense of worthlessness vis-à-vis the Spaniards, he is her most beloved, favored child. As she continues to reassure him, Juan Diego gradually develops a sense of his own dignity as a child of God. In their first encounter, she commanded Juan Diego to ask the Spanish bishop in Mexico City to build a church on the hill where she had appeared. Juan Diego resisted, arguing that he was not worthy to be charged with such a mission. The Lady insisted, so Juan Diego eventually went to the bishop's palace to make the request. At first, the bishop would not even receive the poor indigenous man. Later, the bishop received but did not believe him. Finally, the Lady gave Juan Diego a "sign" to take with him, a bouquet of flowers she had ordered him to pick from a nearby hilltop. Since everyone knew that such flowers could not grow at that time of the year, all who saw the flowers would recognize the miraculous nature of the sign. So Juan Diego put the flowers in his cloak. When the indigenous man arrived at the bishop's palace and opened the cloak to reveal the flowers, another miraculous sign appeared, an image of the Virgin imprinted on the cloak. Stirred and convinced by these signs, the bishop relented and ordered that the Lady's wish be granted.

In addition to signaling a semiotic reversal, where the dark-skinned Lady and the indigenous man become the messengers of God, evangelizers to the Spanish Catholic bishop, the narrative and accompanying images also exemplify a fascinating religious, semiotic *mestizaje*. Tepeyac, the hill on which the Virgin appeared, was well known to the Nahuas (the indigenous people to whom Juan Diego belonged) as the place where they worshiped the mother goddess Tonantzín. Likewise, the Virgin's clothing was adorned with a mixture of Christian and Nahua symbols.[39]

According to Virgilio Elizondo, the Mexican nation as we now know it could not have emerged if not for the Guadalupe event. In 1531, the indigenous peoples of Mexico had been destroyed by the conquering Spaniards; those who had survived the onslaught were demoralized and in despair. At this very moment of deepest anguish, Our Lady of Guadalupe appeared, to accompany them in their suffering, confirm them in their dignity as children of God, and herald the dawn of a new era of hope. Indeed, the image of Guadalupe that Juan Diego saw and the image that, to this day, remains emblazoned on the cloak as it appears in the Basilica of Our Lady of Guadalupe in Mexico City is that of a pregnant woman (unique in the history of Marian apparitions): *La Morenita* gave birth to a new people, a mestizo people. Moreover, Guadalupe's ability to relate the Christian faith to the indigenous worldview, adopting and adapting indigenous symbols to the Christian world-view, made possible the evangelization of Mexico.[40]

The image itself is a powerful example of *mestizaje* in that it combines an array of Christian symbols with symbols indigenous to the Amerindian world of Juan Diego. One finds in the image, for example, numerous symbols of new life, a new beginning, and a new birth: the Lady is pictured as pregnant, she is wearing a "maternity band" around her waist, and she bears on her womb the symbol which, for the Nahuas, represented the "reconciliation of opposites."[41] The most obvious symbol, of course, is the very color of the Lady's skin. To Western Christians accustomed to images of a blonde and blue-eyed Mary, this Lady must surely appear incongruous; her olive skin tells the indigenous people of Mexico that she, *La Morenita*, is one of them. It tells all Mexicans and, indeed, all Latinos that she is one of them. This identity between the Lady and her children is powerfully symbolized by her eyes, in which are reflected the image of Juan Diego himself.[42]

The symbolism and narrative thus reflect the history of Mexico and Latin America as a mestizo people, a rich mixture of different races and cultures. In the figures of *La Morenita* and Juan Diego, God becomes identified with those peoples, cultures, and races who have been marginalized and rejected, Turner's "savages" beyond the frontier/border. Guadalupe represents God's affirmation of the inherent dignity of those whom the European conquerors had deemed to be godless heathens. If Juan Diego is to be evangelized, it will be through a dark-skinned Lady on Tepeyac, the sacred place of the Nahuas, not through a Spanish bishop in his palace. Indeed, through Guadalupe, the very relationship between evangelizer and evangelized is reversed: the indigenous man, Juan Diego, is sent to evangelize the bishop. The traditional roles are thereby reversed: the dark-skinned Lady and the indigenous man themselves become the messengers of God, evangelizers to the Spanish Catholic bishop, who is portrayed as the one in need of conversion. The true missionary is not the bishop but Juan Diego. If the bishop had brought the God of conquest to the Americas, Juan Diego brings the God of the poor, the God of Galilee to the Spanish bishop.

By revealing a Christian God with a special predilection for Juan Diego and his people, Guadalupe thus makes possible the evangelization of America. Without Guadalupe there would be no Mexico. Without the hope engendered by *La Morenita* and her message, Mexico would not have emerged, like the phoenix, from the ashes of the conquest. This direct, historical connection between Guadalupe and Mexican identity is an important source of the passion with which her people celebrate and venerate *La Morenita*. In Guadalupe, the Mexican people have come to know the reality and power of Christ's resurrection, not as an abstract belief, but as a historical reality—a reality once again encountered in Galilee, transforming that land from a frontier into a genuine border. Those who dwell in the borderland are revealed as children of God, the privileged bearers of the good news.

Our Lady of Guadalupe, Juan Diego, Pope John Paul II, and, above all, the crucified and risen Jew from Galilee thus challenge us today to reject the frontier myth that erects fences at the border, that views the border as the meeting point between savagery and civilization. They call us, instead, to go to the border, for there "we will see him"; there we will see the crucified and risen Christ and the dark-skinned Virgin. How we view the border and its inhabitants, then, is not merely a question of charity or justice (though it is that); it is, more profoundly still, a question of our own salvation, our own liberation. Let us not once again, then, like Bishop Juan de Zumárraga five centuries ago, turn away Juan Diego as he approaches us bearing in his tilma the precious gift of God's great love for all of us.

THE WAY, THE TRUTH, AND THE LIFE IN AN AGE OF GLOBALIZATION

In a world where the most vital Christian communities are living alongside and in the midst of other religions, and where, therefore, Christians are becoming increasingly aware of the inescapable fact of religious and cultural pluralism, the particularity of Jesus' identity and claims have important implications for the possibility of living as Christians in a profoundly pluralistic global context. The central question posed to Christians by this context is: How can we affirm the truth of Jesus Christ while affirming the value and desirability of pluralism? David Tracy aptly explains the dilemma:

> In a culture of pluralism must each religious tradition finally either dissolve into some lowest common denominator or accept a marginal existence as one interesting but purely private option? Neither alternative is acceptable to anyone seriously committed to the truth of any major religious tradition. The need is to form a new and inevitably complex theological strategy that will avoid privatism by articulating the genuine

claims of religion to truth. For those in any religious tradition who reject pluralism, such a complex strategy will be deemed unnecessary. Rather the truth of one's own monism can be restated over and over again in the hope that this messy pluralism will one day go away. . . . For those like the present author who accept pluralism as a fundamental enrichment of the human condition, hope must lie elsewhere. But where? A simple affirmation of pluralism can mask a repressive tolerance where all is allowed because nothing is finally taken seriously. Or pluralism can offer a genial confusion. To affirm pluralism responsibly must include an affirmation of truth and public criteria for that affirmation.[43]

A theological aesthetics from the borderland suggests a way out of this dilemma by locating the roots of an authentic pluralism at the heart of the Christian truth itself—that is, by identifying the Way, the Truth, and the Life that is Jesus Christ with the affirmation of human otherness and difference, with the affirmation of the border as a place of encounter between differences rather than a frontier of expansion and conquest. Taking the humanity of Christ seriously means taking the borderland seriously as a privileged *locus theologicus*, as the place where we encounter "the newness of Jesus' vision."

Thus far, I have argued that U.S. Latino/a popular Catholicism represents a *ressourcement* from the margins inasmuch as it retrieves the Catholic tradition "from the underside," making available in a contemporary context aspects of that tradition that have been obscured by modern and postmodern Western culture. Such a retrieval is an important resource for engaging the challenges represented by globalization. More specifically, a liberating theological aesthetics from the borderland is the most appropriate for affirming the normative claims of the crucified and risen Christ in the context of a world church.

The borderland as social location provides an alternative reading of the process of globalization itself. Enrique Dussel notes that, when viewed from the border, the roots of the globalization process can be traced to the conquest of the Americas in 1492, an event that, Dussel argues, signaled the birth of the modern period:

Amerindia is part of "Modernity" from the moment of the conquest and colonization (the mestizo world in Latin America is the only one as old as Modernity), since it is the first "barbarian" which Modernity needs in order to define itself. . . . European Modernity is not an *independent*, autopoietic, self-referring system, rather it is a "part" of the "world-system": its *center*. Modernity, then, is a phenomenon that globalizes itself; it begins with the *simultaneous* constitution of Spain with reference to its "periphery." . . . *Simultaneously*, Europe . . . will *constitute itself* as center over a growing "periphery."[44]

Globalization thus begins, not with the relativization of borders, but, on the contrary, with the creation of a frontier that will separate "civilization" from "barbarism"; the frontier is central not only to U.S. identity but to modern Western identity beginning with Columbus. From its very origins and of its very essence, modernity needs and demands a center and a periphery, separated by a border (frontier); conquest is not the consequence but the origin of modernity. "Before the rest of Europe," writes Dussel, "[Spain and Portugal] subjected the Other to conquest and to the dominion of the *center* over the *periphery*. Europe then established itself as the 'center' of the world (in the planetary sense) and brought forth modernity and its myth."[45] The Cartesian individualism and rationalism so often associated with the origins of modernity are, conversely, merely derivative, legitimating consequences of the center-periphery global structure:

The "rationalization" of political life (bureaucratization), of capitalist enterprise (administration), of everyday life (Calvinist or Puritan asceticism), the disembodiment of subjectivity . . . , the non-ethical character of every economic or political action (understood exclusively as technical engineering), the suppression of practical-communicative reason replaced by instrumental reason, the solipsistic individualism which denies community, etc., . . . are *effects* of the realization of that function proper to Europe as "center" of the world-system.[46]

Though not always as manifestly or explicitly as during the conquest of the Americas, religion has played and will continue to play a crucial role in the process of globalization. Today, cultural and economic globalization is accompanied by a resurgence of religious fervor, especially in the third world. This fervor, which represents a resistance to the forces of globalization, often takes fundamentalist or even violent forms. Neither the muticulturalism promised by postmodern prophets of ambiguity, otherness, and difference, nor the economic-technological liberation promised by the proponents of globalization has seemed to materialize. Indeed, third-world peoples are becoming increasingly restive and defiant in the face of such promises.

At stake is precisely the existence and character of the border as a place of encounter. Christian theology must be able to articulate what the nature of that encounter will be, and a U.S. Latino/a liberation theological aesthetics, with the crucified and risen Christ at its center, brings important resources to that theological task. As I have previously suggested, that task will be liberating only insofar as it resists both the postmodern absolutization of particularity and the modern negation of particularity (or absolutization of one single particularity, the European).

THE EUCHARIST IN AN AGE OF GLOBALIZATION: LIBERATION AND AESTHETICS RECONCILED

Likewise, a theological aesthetics from the borderland must resist the temptation to pit liberation and U.S. Hispanic theologies over against theological aesthetics as if the former were a liberal reduction of faith to social action and the latter a conservative preservation of the transcendence of the Christian God against precisely such a reduction. Such a simplistic dichotomy misconstrues both liberation theology and theological aesthetics. Indeed, the preferential option for the poor safeguards the transcendence of God over against those theologies which, either implicitly or explicitly, would identify God with the status quo thereby absolutizing the regnant social order, turning it into an idol. The attempt to reconcile liberation theology with theological aesthetics is at the heart of the theological task in a global context, for that task must include the attempt to reconcile the affirmation of particularity, or otherness, with the possibility of making normative truth claims.

If God is transcendent, outside our world order, then God will be encountered among those persons who, as victims of our world order, have been excluded from participating and, thus, remain invisible to that world order. (Conversely, the transcendent God will be as invisible in that world as are those persons who have been excluded.) Any religious worship, therefore, that does not begin on the periphery, among the excluded victims of the world order, can only be worship of an idol, a god who legitimates the system of domination either explicitly (e.g., the conquest) or implicitly (e.g., a privatized, individualistic faith). True worship originates in "liberative praxis with respect to and for the oppressed in whom one recognizes the epiphany of infinite Exteriority."[47] If the transcendent God is encountered, first, on the cross, then all those persons who continue to be crucified today must be the starting point of Christian theological reflection and worship. This, indeed, has been at the heart of my argument: as the religious and spiritual practices of a marginalized people, U.S. Latino/a popular Catholicism is a form of worship that makes possible a liberating encounter with the transcendent God, "infinite Exteriority."

The intrinsic connection between the struggle for justice and worship of a transcendent God is nowhere more evident than in the Christian community's central form of worship, the eucharistic liturgy, for the Eucharist itself is always at the same time a religious act and an economic act, always at the same time an aesthetic reception of the "One who loved us first" and, in the most materially concrete form possible (bread and wine), a prophetic denunciation of our own refusal to love. The eucharistic bread is at the same time "the substance of the eucharistic offering" and "the fruit of common human labor, exchanged among those who produce it."[48] (Or, as we proclaim in the eucharistic liturgy, the bread and wine are "fruit of the earth and work of human hands.") Since the bread is "the objectivized life of the worker" whose labor makes possible our liturgical celebration, "those who offer God bread stolen from the poor give God the life of the poor as their offering."[49]

This connection between liberating praxis and aesthetic receptivity, between justice and worship is powerfully made manifest in the life of the Spanish missionary Bartolomé de Las Casas. Arriving in the New World as an *encomendero* (slaveowner), Las Casas was eventually ordained a priest, joined the Dominican order, and committed himself to the evangelization of the Indians. Though known for his charitable treatment of the Indians in his care, Las Casas nevertheless did not initially see a contradiction between his Christian, priestly calling and his role as an *encomendero*. This viewpoint changed when, while preparing to celebrate the eucharistic liturgy one day, the Spanish Dominican underwent a conversion that would dramatically alter his understanding of his Christian faith, his priestly vocation, his role as a missionary, and, especially, his relationship with the indigenous peoples of America. While studying the Scriptures in preparation for his homily, Las Casas came across a text from the book of Sirach (34:18-22):

> Tainted his gifts who offers in sacrifice ill-gotten
>   goods!
> Mock presents from the lawless win not God's favor.
> The Most High approves not the gifts of the godless.
> [Nor for their many sacrifices does he forgive their
>   sins.]
> Like the man who slays a son in his father's presence
> is he who offers sacrifice from the possessions
>   of the poor.
> The bread of charity is life itself for the needy,
> he who withholds it is a person of blood.
> He slays his neighbor who deprives him of his living;
> he sheds blood who denies the laborer his wages.[50]

This text opened Las Casas's eyes to the meaning and import of the liturgical action he was about to undertake. As a slaveowner, he would be offering to God bread and wine that were the fruit of the labor of the Amerindians in his care, men and women who themselves remained poor and hungry. In the Holy Sacrifice of the Mass, he would be offering to God the "objectivized lives" of his workers; he would be sacrificing *their* lives on God's altar, thereby committing the worst kind of sacrilege and blasphemy. Any God who would countenance and accept such a sacrifice could not be the transcendent, just God of the Scriptures but a mere idol, a "god" who legitimates murder.[51]

This realization led to Las Casas's subsequent decision to release his slaves, himself becoming a tireless defender of the Amerindians.[52] If the Spanish conquistadores and missionaries condemned the Indians for their practice of human sacrifice, he argued, the Spanish Christians themselves were guilty of human sacrifice when, in the Mass, they presented their offerings of bread and wine, products of the blood, sweat, and tears extracted from the indigenous peoples of the Americas. If the Amerindians did not accept the message preached by the Spanish missionaries, such recalcitrance was not only understandable but justifiable and, indeed, demanded; what the Amerindians rejected was not the God of love preached by the Spanish but the god of hatred and violence manifested in their actions. In that context, the Indians not only had a right to reject "Christianity" but a duty to do so, for what they were rejecting was not Christianity but an idolatry more destructive than the idolatry practiced by the indigenous peoples themselves.[53]

As Las Casas had so prophetically argued, if at the very heart of the Christian faith is the assertion that "God is love," a genuine respect for and love of the other is a condition of the possibility for any authentic evangelization. In other words, an authentically intersubjective praxis is the fundamental criterion of the credibility and validity of the Christian faith, and of Christian worship: "everyone who loves is begotten of God and has knowledge of God. . . . God is love, and he who abides in love abides in God, and God in him" (1 John 4:7, 16).

This understanding of Christian faith has implications for the possibility of asserting Christian truth in our postmodern, globalized, pluralistic context. If the central Christian truth is precisely that "God is love" (i.e., God is intersubjective praxis), then that truth is validated when and where one finds true respect for and dialogue with the other. Conversely, where such intersubjectivity is absent, regardless of any express claims, the truth of Christianity is being denied. Paradoxically, then, a genuine openness to non-Christians and, a fortiori, to non-European Christians is a necessary precondition for Christian evangelization and the development of a truly global Christianity, a world church. Truth is constitutively and essentially intersubjective, communitarian.[54]

To see the form of the crucified and risen Christ on the border is to recognize the intrinsically intercultural and, indeed, interreligious character of that form. In the twenty-first century, one cannot do Christian theology without daring to breach cultural, religious, racial, gender, economic, and other borders that prevent us from encountering the God who approaches us from the other side. Conversely, to pretend that the truth of Christ can be known or, even worse, can only be known in some pure form unsullied by external influences is the most fundamental denial of that very truth; it would be to crucify Christ all over again.

MATERIALITY, RELIGION, AND GLOBALIZATION: TOWARD A TRANSMODERN CHRISTIANITY

Because religious and cultural intersubjectivity is always also material, socioeconomic intersubjectivity, such encounters presuppose the existence of just material relationships among the participants: genuine encounters and dialogue are impossible between master and slave, between a conquistador bearing firearms and an unarmed Aztec woman, between a wealthy person (who refuses to surrender his or her wealth) and a poor person, or between a Christianity backed by economic and political power and thirdworld religions or cultures without access to such resources. In other words, while the normative claims of a theological aesthetics (i.e., the gratuity of God's love) ground theologically the struggle for justice, this latter always historically mediates a Christian theological aesthetics. There can be no beauty without justice; the gratuity of God's love can only be experienced in and through the struggle for justice—even if that justice receives its fullest meaning only in the form of gratuity, mercy, reconciliation, and worship. All human relationships, including those specifically and explicitly religious in character, have material mediations; our relationships always take place within determinate cultural, political, racial, religious, gender, and economic structures, all of which inform those relationships. Postmodern discourse on otherness and difference remains inevitably abstract if it remains inattentive, not only to the cultural, racial, gender, and religious mediations of otherness, but, even more concretely, to its socioeconomic mediations—which are also implied in the others.[55] If religion and, a fortiori, liberating religion is concerned with human life, it must be concerned with that life in its utter historical concreteness—namely, in its materiality and corporeality. The spiritual, religious, transcendent character of the person is always mediated by (not reduced to or identified with) socioeconomic relationships. These latter necessarily influence (not "determine") the former.

An authentic globalization, which would allow and respect both the particularity of different cultures and their common claim to universality (not just the claim to universality of European cultures), means much more than simply an openness to other points of views and religious traditions. Such a globalization presupposes a just global economic order, one that would foster the participation of all peoples. In fact, argues Dussel, the contemporary understanding of globalization in the West promotes an affective openness while simultaneously fostering and legitimating the active exclusion of billions of human beings from the economic order. Paradoxically, such globalization and exclusion go hand in hand. Dussel notes,

> One should not forget that the final or macro context of this *Ethics* [of Liberation] is the process of *globalization*; but, unfortunately and simultaneously, that process is the *exclusion* of the great majority of humanity: the victims of the world-system. Globalization-Exclusion refers to the double movement in which the global Periphery finds itself caught: on the one hand, the presumed modernization within the formal globalization of capital . . . ; but, on the other hand, the material exclusion . . . of the victims of that presumed civilizing process.[56]

The starting point for any process of globalization that would pretend to promote a genuine pluralism among world cultures and religions must thus be a particular sociohistorical locus—namely, that of the "*excluídos*," those residents of the borderlands who have been excluded from participation in our presumed global community. "In the victim, dominated or excluded by the system," asserts Dussel, "concrete, empirical, living human subjectivity is revealed, it appears in the last instance as an 'appeal': it is the subject who now can-not-live and cries from pain. It is the appeal of the one who exclaims: 'I am hungry!' 'Feed me, please!'"[57]

In short, an authentic globalization presupposes a praxis of liberation that takes as its starting point the *vida cotidiana*, the everyday suffering and struggles of the victim (of a dominative, false globalization), and seeks a transformation of those social structures that deny the victim his or her historical agency as a human subject. In other words, the condition of the possibility for creating a truly reconciled community wherein a dialogue among equals can effectively take place is the liberation of those peoples who today remain excluded from participation in such dialogue because they are not deemed to be full historical subjects. The precondition for such global equality is, paradoxically, a preferential option for the victims: "The person who functions critico-ethically *should* (is obliged to) liberate the victim, as a participant (due to the 'situation' or 'position', Gramsci would say) in the same community to which the victim belongs. . . . This obligation has a universal claim; that is, it is true for every act and in every human situation."[58]

Beyond the equally dichotomous and abstract worldviews of modernity and postmodernity, therefore, Enrique Dussel offers a third possibility, the "transmodern." While modernity and postmodernity presuppose the same dichotomous, dualistic epistemology, *trans*modernity is characterized by a holistic, organic epistemology rooted in the act of solidarity with the victims of history. Precisely because, as opposed to the operative paradigms (or myths) of modernity and postmodernity, the notion of transmodernity refers not so much to a new way of thinking as to a new way of living in relation to others, transmodernity rejects the subject-object dichotomy underlying both the modern and postmodern paradigms.

Likewise, the transmodern paradigm that Dussel proposes rejects both the conceptualist rationalism of modernity and the irrationalism of poststructuralist postmodernism. Instead, transmodernity makes possible the retrieval and revaluation of the excluded cultures, the cultures and lives of the victims precisely as rational:

I seek to overcome modernity not through a postmodern attack on reason based on the irrational incommensurability of language-games. Rather, I propose a transmodern opposition to modernity's irrational violence based on the *reason of the Other*. . . . The Other encompasses the peripheral colonial world, the sacrificed Indian, the enslaved black, the oppressed woman, the subjugated child, and the alienated popular culture—all victims of modernity's irrational action in contradiction to its own rational ideal. . . . The discovery of the ethical dignity of the Other purifies Enlightenment rationality beyond any Eurocentric or developmentalist communicative reason and certainly beyond purely strategic, instrumental rationality. . . . Thus I hope to transcend modern reason not by negating reason as such, but by negating violent, Eurocentric, developmentalist, hegemonic reason. . . . The transmodern project achieves with modernity what it could not achieve by itself—a corealization of solidarity, which is analectic, analogic, syncretic, hybrid, and mestizo. . . .[59]

Concretely, then, what are the implications of Dussel's argument for religion and, more specifically, for Christianity in an age of globalization? What might a transmodern Christianity look like? What seems clear is that, whatever the answer to those questions, they will not be found primarily in the places and among those groups that have heretofore—or, at least, in the last five centuries—defined Christianity. No longer can we assume that the center of the Christian world is in the North Atlantic. A transmodern Christianity will privilege one particular social location—the borderland—whose residents, as *excluídos*, most fully reveal the "absolutely absolute Other," thereby safeguarding the transcendence of God over against the ever-present tendency to identify God with historical success and conquest. The Christianity of the twenty-first century will be defined above all by precisely those excluded peoples who represent the underside of the much-vaunted globalization currently under way. Whatever the wishes and expectations of ecclesiastical elites and their epigones, the Christianity of the future will increasingly look like the Christianity of third-world peoples (whether these live in their native countries or have immigrated to first-world countries).

A Christianity that takes seriously the challenge of an authentic globalization will reject the impenetrable barriers that North Atlantic Christianity has erected between the saved and the damned, between civilization and savagery. If borders between cultures, religions, and nations are necessary to preserve particular identities, those borders will nevertheless allow for mutual interaction.[60] When a border thus conceived functions as a privileged *locus theologicus* for Christian theology, the Way, the Truth, and the Life revealed therein will be intrinsically practical and intersubjective. The borderland reveals a truth that is normative and universal precisely *because* it is intersubjective and particular. The universal truth revealed in Jesus Christ is, paradoxically, the truth of the intrinsically intersubjective foundation of all reality. It is in the borderland particularity of *this* person, Jesus of Nazareth, that we encounter the universal truth revealed in the person of Jesus Christ: God is love. As Las Casas so courageously avowed, any form of Christianity that allows or legitimates exclusion and domination is, ipso facto, a denial of the very truth it professes and, de facto, an example of idol worship. A truly global Christianity is thus a Christianity that allows for the crossing of borders (not the elimination of borders), thereby affirming in practice the belief that truth is intersubjective, that God is love.

By insisting on the concrete, historical mediation of otherness in the face of the victim and, hence, in the concrete, historical mediation of the "absolutely absolute Other," a liberating theological aesthetics empowers us to reread history from its underside and, thus, to move beyond the false alternatives posed by modern and postmodern cultures. Those false alternatives have yielded a globalization made possible only by excluding literally billions of human beings from full participation, as equals, in the globalization process. An authentic transmodern globalization, one that is truly pluralistic, demands that the process be initiated, not from within the centers of power, but from the margins, from the borderland. And it is precisely there, among the residents of the borderland, that Christians will encounter the liberating God who loved us first.

Notes

PREFACE

[1]I find particularly troubling, for example, certain assumptions about gender roles and his understanding of the character of those roles—what is often called "essentializing." For a critical analysis of these issues, see Michelle A. Gonzalez, "Hans Urs von Balthasar and Contemporary Feminist Theology," *Theological Studies* 65 (September 2004): 566-595.

1. PROCLAIMING THE TRUTH OF CHRIST IN THE TWENTY-FIRST CENTURY

[1]John Paul II, "Ecclesia in Europa," June 28, 2003, para. 14.

[2]John Paul II, *Fides et Ratio*, September 14, 1998, para. 32.

[3]Benedict XVI, *Spe Salvi*, November 30, 2007, para. 8.

[4]Juan Luis Segundo, *Faith and Ideologies* (Eugene, Ore.: Wipf and Stock, 2006).

[5]Jon Sobrino, *Where Is God? Earthquake, Terrorism, Barbarity, and Hope* (Maryknoll, N.Y.: Orbis Books, 2004), 73.

[6]John Paul II, *Dilecti Amici*, March 31, 1985, para. 7.

[7]Jon Sobrino, *Spirituality of Liberation* (Maryknoll, N.Y.: Orbis Books, 1988), 166-167.

[8]Ignacio Ellacuría, "Las iglesias latinoamericanas interpelan a la iglesia de Espana," *Sal Terrae* (March 1982), 224 (my translation).

[9]Hans Urs Von Balthasar, *Truth Is Symphonic* (San Francisco: Ignatius Press, 1987), 64.

[10]Diego Irarrazaval, *Inculturation: New Dawn of the Church in Latin America* (Maryknoll, N.Y.: Orbis Books, 2000), 91.

[11]Sobrino, *Spirituality of Liberation*, 171.

[12]Ibid., 166-167.

[13]Quoted in José Ignacio González Faus, *La interpelación de las iglesias latinoamericanas a la Europa postmoderna y a las iglesias europeas* (Madrid: Colegio Mayor Chaminade, 1988), 121-122 (my translation).

[14]Ibid., 124.

[15]Ernest Becker, *The Denial of Death* (New York: Free Press, 1973).

[16]Not exclusively Christian, moreover, this is also the message of the Buddha, Siddhartha Gautama. In the famous story of his childhood, Siddhartha's path to enlightenment did not begin until he was able to escape the luxurious compound in which he had been raised and, once outside its walls, came face to face with a corpse, a beggar, and a sick person—the "three sights" of human mortality. Having seen himself mirrored in those persons, and recognizing that he himself would eventually become like them, he decided to leave behind his luxurious lifestyle in search of enlightenment. Like Siddhartha's face-to-face encounter with human mortality, Thomas's act of placing his hand into Jesus' side brought him face to face with his own weakness and powerlessness, and with his own sinful participation in the acts that inflicted the wounds. For Thomas and the disciples, as for Siddhartha, their conversion began with the recognition that, in the words of Martin Luther, "We are *all* beggars."

[17]Johann Baptist Metz, *Faith in History and Society: Toward a Practical Fundamental Theology* (New York: Seabury Press, 1980), 109.

[18]Walter Benjamin, quoted in David Tracy, *Plurality and Ambiguity: Hermeneutics, Religion, Hope* (San Francisco: Harper and Row, 1987), 69.

[19]González Faus, *Interpelación*, 111.

[20]Justo González, *Santa Biblia: The Bible through Hispanic Eyes* (Nashville: Abingdon Press, 1996), 85-86.

[21]Justo González, *Mañana: Christian Theology from a Hispanic Perspective* (Nashville: Abingdon Press, 1990), 40.

[22]Ibid., 39.

[23]Ibid.

[24]Ibid., 40.

2. RECONCILIATION IN CHRIST

[1]*Boston Globe*, April 14, 2006.

[2]Ibid., April 15, 2006.

[3]For a more extended treatment of this analysis of the resurrection, see my "The Crucified and Risen Christ: From Calvary to Galilee," *Proceedings of the Catholic Theological Society of America*, vol. 60, 57-71, an abridged version of which was also published in the April 17, 2006, issue of *America*.

[4]James Alison, *Knowing Jesus* (Springfield, Ill.: Templegate, 1994), 83.

[5]Daniel M. Bell Jr., *Liberation Theology after the End of History:*

The Refusal to Cease Suffering (London: Routledge, 2001), 152.

[6]Franz Hinkelammert, cited in ibid.

[7]Bell, *Liberation Theology*, 152-153.

[8]Ibid., 153.

[9]Gustavo Gutiérrez, *On Job: God-Talk and the Suffering of the Innocent* (Maryknoll, N.Y.: Orbis Books, 1987), 87-88.

[10]Cited in Bell, *Liberation Theology*, 178.

[11]Ibid.

[12]Jon Sobrino, *The Principle of Mercy: Taking the Crucified People from the Cross* (Maryknoll, N.Y.: Orbis Books, 1994), 92.

[13]Ibid., 96.

[14]Ibid., 89-90.

[15]Bell, *Liberation Theology*, 174.

[16]Sobrino, *Principle of Mercy*, 159-160.

[17]Bell, *Liberation Theology*, 182-183, 188.

[18]Ibid., 164.

[19]Gutiérrez, *On Job*, xiii.

[20]Bell, *Liberation Theology*, 195.

[21]Gutiérrez, *On Job*, 103.

[22]Bell, *Liberation Theology*, 195.

[23]Gustavo Gutiérrez, *The Density of the Present: Selected Writings* (Maryknoll, N.Y.: Orbis Books, 1999), 141.

[24]Sobrino, *Principle of Mercy*, 96.

[25]Bell, *Liberation Theology*, 168.

[26]José Ellacuría, quoted in ibid., 171.

[27]Douglas John Hall, *The Cross in Our Context: Jesus and the Suffering World* (Minneapolis: Fortress, 2003), 140.

[28]Alison, *Knowing Jesus*, 81.

[29]Ibid., 82.

[30]Jon Sobrino, *The True Church and the Poor* (Maryknoll, N.Y.: Orbis Books, 1984), 93.

[31]Ibid., 96.

[32]M. Shawn Copeland, "The Church Is Marked by Suffering," in *The Many Marks of the Church*, ed. William Madges and Michael J. Daley (New London, Conn.: Twenty-Third Publications, 2006), 214.

[33]Ibid., 216.

[34]Henri de Lubac, *Corpus Mysticum: l'eucharistie et l'Église au Moyen âge. Étude historique* (Paris: Aubier, 1949).

[35]Joseph Ratzinger, *The Spirit of the Liturgy* (San Francisco: Ignatius Press, 2000), 88.

[36]Gustavo Gutiérrez, *We Drink from Our Own Wells: The Spiritual Journey of a People* (Maryknoll, N.Y.: Orbis Books, 1984), 69.

[37]Kevin F. Burke, "Christian Salvation and the Disposition of Tran-

scendence: Ignacio Ellacuría's Historical Soteriology," in *Love That Produces Hope: The Thought of Ignacio Ellacuría*, ed. Kevin F. Burke and Robert Lassalle-Klein (Collegeville, Minn.: Liturgical Press, 2006), 179-180.

[38]The significance of corporeality—and of the connection between christological and anthropological corporeality--for the ongoing struggles of women, especially, has been developed by a number of scholars. For instance, see María Clara Bingemer, "Women in the Future of the Theology of Liberation," in *Feminist Theology from the Third World*, ed. Ursula King (London: SPCK, 1994); Elisabeth Moltmann-Wendel, *I Am My Body: A Theology of Embodiment* (New York: Continuum, 1995); and Sallie McFague, *The Body of God: An Ecological Theology* (Minneapolis: Fortress, 1993).

[39]Burke, "Christian Salvation and the Disposition of Transcendence," 178.

[40]Alison, *Knowing Jesus*, 84.

[41]Ibid., 92.

3. POPULAR CATHOLICISM

[1]Diego Irarrazaval, *Rito y Pensar Cristiano* (Lima: Centro de Estudios y Publicaciones, 1993), 146. This and all subsequent quotations from this book are my translations.

[2]Ibid., 154.

[3]John Paul II, *Ecclesia in America*, January 22, 1999, para. 16; quote is from *Propositio* 21.

[4]Keith Pecklers, S.J., *Liturgia en contexto* (Caracas, Venezuela: Paulinas Editorial, 2005), 162. This and all subsequent quotations from this book are my translations.

[5]Ibid., 36.

[6]Ibid., 48.

[7]Ibid., 164-165.

[8]Ibid., 167.

[9]Martin D. Stringer, *A Sociological History of Christian Worship* (Cambridge: Cambridge University Press, 2005), 235.

[10]See, e.g., "Changing Faiths: Latinos and the Transformation of American Religion," Pew Hispanic Center and Pew Forum on Religion and Public Life, April 25, 2007, http://pewhispanic.org/files/reports/75. pdf.

[11]See Alejandro García-Rivera, *St. Martín de Porres: The "Little Stories" and the Semiotics of Culture* (Maryknoll, N.Y.: Orbis Books, 1995).

[12]Pecklers, *Liturgia en contexto*, 34.

[13]Ibid., 170-171.

[14]Ibid., 48.

[15]Ibid., 171.

[16]William A. Christian Jr., "Spain in Latino Religiosity," in *El Cuerpo de Cristo: The Hispanic Presence in the U.S. Catholic Church*, ed. Peter Casarella and Raúl Gómez (New York: Crossroad, 1998), 326-327.

[17]Ibid., 327.

[18]Gary Macy, "Demythologizing 'the Church' in the Middle Ages," *Journal of Hispanic/Latino Theology* 3, no. 1 (August 1995): 27.

[19]Orlando Espín, *Faith of the People: Theological Reflections on Popular Catholicism* (Maryknoll, N.Y.: Orbis Books, 1997), 117.

[20]Ibid., 119.

[21]Orlando Espín, "Pentecostalism and Popular Catholicism: The Poor and *Traditio*," *Journal of Hispanic/Latino Theology* 3, no. 2 (November 1995): 19.

[22]María Rosa Menocal, *La joya del mundo: musulmanes, judíos y cristianos, y la cultura de la tolerancia en al-Andalus* (Barcelona: Plaza y Janés, 2004), 24. This and all subsequent quotations from this book are my translations.

[23]Espín, "Pentecostalism and Popular Catholicism," 19.

[24]Mark Francis, "Popular Piety and Liturgical Reform in a Hispanic Context," in *Dialogue Rejoined: Theology and Ministry in the United States Hispanic Reality*, ed. Ana María Pineda and Robert Schreiter (Collegeville, Minn.: Liturgical Press, 1995), 165-166.

[25]Avery Dulles, *Models of the Church* (Garden City, N.Y.: Doubleday, 1987), 36; quoted in Gary Macy, "Demythologizing 'the Church' in the Middle Ages," *Journal of Hispanic/Latino Theology* 3, no. 1 (August 1995): 27.

[26]Macy, "Demythologizing," 27.

[27]Ibid., 27-32.

[28]Ibid., 31-32, 38.

[29]Ibid., 35.

[30]Ibid.

[31]Francis, "Popular Piety," 166.

[32]Macy, "Demythologizing," 35-37.

[33]Ibid., 40.

[34]Louis Dupré, *Passage to Modernity: An Essay in the Hermeneutics of Nature and Culture* (New Haven, Conn.: Yale University Press, 1995), 94.

[35]Caroline Bynum, "Why All the Fuss about the Body? A Medievalist's Perspective," in *Beyond the Cultural Turn: New Directions in the*

Study of Society and Culture, ed. Victoria Bonnell et al. (Berkeley: University of California Press, 1999), 251-252.

[36]Ibid.

[37]Dupré, *Passage to Modernity*, 3.

[38]Ibid., 179.

[39]Ibid., 163-164.

[40]Karl Rahner, "The Theology of the Symbol," in Rahner, *Theological Investigations IV* (New York: Crossroad, 1966), 244.

[41]Irarrazaval, *Rito y Pensar Cristiano*, 98.

[42]Thomas F. O'Meara, *Theology of Ministry* (New York: Paulist Press, 1999), 115-116.

[43]Robert A. Orsi, *Thank You, St. Jude: Women's Devotion to the Patron Saint of Hopeless Causes* (New Haven, Conn.: Yale University Press, 1996), 33-34.

[44]Espín, "Pentecostalism and Popular Catholicism," 26.

[45]Vincent J. Miller, *Consuming Religion: Christian Faith and Practice in a Consumer Culture* (New York: Continuum, 2004), 11.

[46]Ibid., 6.

[47]Ibid., 25.

[48]Ibid., 64.

[49]Ibid., 69-70.

[50]Ibid., 84.

[51]Ibid.

[52]Ibid., 91.

[53]Ibid., 138-139.

[54]Ibid., 202.

[55]Ibid.

[56]Thomas Groome, *What Makes Us Catholic: Eight Gifts for Life* (San Francisco: HarperCollins, 2002), 84-85.

[57]Irarrazaval, *Rito y Pensar Cristiano*, 138.

[58]Puebla Documents, No. 465 (quoted in ibid., 24).

[59]Irarrazaval, *Rito y Pensar Cristiano*, 39.

4. HISTORICAL PRAXIS AS CHRISTOPRAXIS

[1]Peter Casarella, "Questioning the Primacy of Method: On Sokolowski's *Eucharistic Presence*," *Communio* 22 (Winter 1995): 670-671.

[2]Ibid., 669.

[3]Ibid., 675.

[4]Ibid., 700.

[5]Thomas Aquinas, *Summa Theologiae*, 1-2, q.1a.

[6]Thomas Merton, *Conjectures of a Guilty Bystander* (Garden City, N.Y.: Doubleday, 1966), 265.

⁷Hence the reaction I received from Jesús in that Chicago parish (see the Introduction to this volume). Even if one can technically describe the Gospels as "narratives," what I think Jesús was rejecting was any latent assumption that the Gospels are merely a subset of a larger genre ("narrative"), point to the same reality as other religious narratives, and are thus interchangeable with those other narratives. I have come to the realization that what matters to the people with whom I have worked in the community and in the parishes is precisely the reality of the Gospels, the reality of Juan Diego, the reality of Guadalupe, the reality of Jesus Christ.

⁸John Paul II, *Fides et Ratio*, para. 97.

⁹Gustavo Gutiérrez, *We Drink from Our Own Wells: The Spiritual Journey of a People* (Maryknoll, N.Y.: Orbis Books, 2003), 38.

¹⁰Ibid., 46.

¹¹Jon Sobrino, *Jesus in Latin America* (Maryknoll, N.Y.: Orbis Books, 1987), 165.

¹²Ibid., 158 (emphasis in original).

¹³I am indebted to Professor Otto Maduro for this insight.

¹⁴Gutiérrez, *We Drink from Our Own Wells*, 48.

¹⁵Ibid., 51.

¹⁶Sobrino, *Spirituality of Liberation* (Maryknoll, N.Y.: Orbis Books, 1988), 70.

¹⁷Ibid., 71.

¹⁸Ibid., 105.

¹⁹Georges Bernanos, quoted in Jean-François Six, *Light of the Night: The Last Eighteen Months in the Life of Thérèse of Lisieux* (Notre Dame, Ind.: University of Notre Dame Press, 1998), 175-176.

²⁰Henri Nouwen, Foreword, in Gutiérrez, *We Drink from Our Own Wells*, xviii.

²¹St. Bonaventure, quoted in John Paul II, *Fides et Ratio*, para. 105.

²²Gustavo Gutiérrez, *A Theology of Liberation: History, Politics, and Salvation* (Maryknoll, N.Y.: Orbis Books, 1988), 11.

²³Gutiérrez, *We Drink from Our Own Wells*, 109-112.

²⁴Gutiérrez, *On Job: God-Talk and the Suffering of the Innocent* (Maryknoll, N.Y.: Orbis Books, 1987), xiii.

²⁵John Paul II, *Veritatis Splendor*, August 6, 1993, para. 10.

²⁶Gutiérrez, *We Drink from Our Own Wells*, 96.

²⁷Gutiérrez, *The Truth Shall Make You Free: Confrontations* (Maryknoll, N.Y.: Orbis Books, 1990), 101.

²⁸James B. Nickoloff, Introduction, in *Gustavo Gutiérrez: Essential Writings*, ed. Nickoloff (Maryknoll, N.Y.: Orbis Books, 1996), 9.

²⁹Gutiérrez, *On Job*, 89.

[30]Diego Irarrazaval, *Rito y Pensar Cristiano* (Lima: Centro de Estudios y Publicaciones, 1993), 17, 161.

[31]Sobrino, *Spirituality of Liberation*, 56-58.

[32]Gutiérrez, *On Job*, xiii.

[33]Aidan Nichols, *No Bloodless Myth: A Guide through Balthasar's Dramatics* (Washington, D.C.: Catholic University of America Press, 2000), 12.

[34]Roberto S. Goizueta, *Caminemos con Jesús: Toward a Hispanic/Latino Theology of Accompaniment* (Maryknoll, N.Y.: Orbis Books, 1995).

[35]Irarrazaval, *Rito y Pensar Cristiano*, 133.

[36]Hans Urs von Balthasar, *Theo-Drama: Theological Dramatic Theory*, 5 vols., trans. Graham Harrison (San Francisco: Ignatius Press, 1988-1998), 1:31-34; also quoted in Nichols, *No Bloodless Myth*, 13.

[37]Ibid., 33-34.

[38]Hans Urs von Balthasar, *Prayer* (San Francisco: Ignatius Press, 1986), 172.

[39]Ibid.

[40]Ibid., 172-173.

5. SEEING THE FORM

[1]Hans Urs von Balthasar, *The Glory of the Lord*, Vol. 1, *Seeing the Form* (San Francisco: Ignatius Press, 1982), 151.

[2]Alejandro García-Rivera, *The Community of the Beautiful: A Theological Aesthetics* (Collegeville, Minn.: Liturgical Press, 1999), 88-89.

[3]Hans Urs von Balthasar, *Truth Is Symphonic: Aspects of Christian Pluralism* (San Francisco: Ignatius Press, 1987), 38.

[4]H. Schlier, quoted in Hans Urs von Balthasar, *Mysterium Paschale: The Mystery of Easter* (San Francisco: Ignatius Press, 1990), 218.

[5]Balthasar, *Mysterium Paschale*, 218.

[6]Ibid., 219.

[7]Balthasar, *Truth Is Symphonic*, 65.

[8]Ibid.

[9]Jon Sobrino, *Spirituality of Liberation* (Maryknoll, N.Y.: Orbis Books, 1988), 69.

[10]Balthasar, quoted in Michelle Gonzalez, *Sor Juana: Beauty and Justice in the Americas* (Maryknoll, N.Y.: Orbis Books, 2003), 177.

[11]Sobrino, *Spirituality of Liberation*, 170.

[12]Balthasar, *Truth Is Symphonic*, 76.

[13]Balthasar, *Glory of the Lord*, 1:437-438.

[14]Gustavo Gutiérrez, *We Drink from Our Own Wells: The Spiritual Journey of a People* (Maryknoll, N.Y.: Orbis Books, 1984), 102-103.

[15]Ibid., 69.

[16]William T. Cavanaugh, *Torture and Eucharist: Theology, Politics, and the Body of Christ* (Oxford: Blackwell, 1998), 233.

[17]James Nickoloff, ed., *Gustavo Gutiérrez: Selected Writings* (Maryknoll, N.Y.: Orbis Books, 1996), 270.

[18]Gustavo Gutiérrez, *A Theology of Liberation: History, Politics, and Salvation* (Maryknoll, N.Y.: Orbis Books, 1988), 206n18.

[19]Balthasar, *Glory of the Lord*, 1:151.

[20]David Bentley Hart, *The Beauty of the Infinite: The Aesthetics of Christian Truth* (Grand Rapids: Eerdmans, 2003), 21.

[21]Ibid., 22.

[22]Quoted in Hans Urs von Balthasar, *The Glory of the Lord*, Vol. 4, *A Theological Aesthetics* (San Francisco: Ignatius Press, 1989), 27n11; also quoted in Hart, *Beauty of the Infinite*, 23.

[23]Hart, *Beauty of the Infinite*, 24-25.

[24]Ibid., 22.

[25]Ibid., 27-28.

[26]Ibid., 20.

[27]Ibid., 19.

[28]Ibid., 344.

[29]Ibid., 339.

[30]Ibid., 20

[31]Hans Urs von Balthasar, quoted in Raymond Gawronski, S.J., *Word and Silence: Hans Urs von Balthasar and the Spiritual Encounter between East and West* (T. & T. Clark, 1995), 136.

[32]Gonzalez, *Sor Juana*, 170-171.

[33]Jon Sobrino, *The Principle of Mercy: Taking the Crucified People from the Cross* (Maryknoll, N.Y.: Orbis Books, 1994), 96.

[34]Hart, *Beauty of the Infinite*, 272-273.

[35]Ibid., 390 (emphasis added).

[36]Indeed, this is a good definition of clinical depression: all reality is essentially wounded, so what is felt is not pain (which can only be experienced as "pain" in relation to some other reality, i.e., "happiness"), but simply numbness.

[37]John Paul II, "Salvifici Doloris," February 11, 1984, para. 21.

[38]Simone Weil, *Gravity and Grace* (London: Routledge, 2002), 145.

6. REIMAGINING THE BORDER

[1]Alfred Lord Tennyson, from "Ulysses," quoted in Frederick Jackson Turner, *Rereading Frederick Jackson Turner*, with commentary by John Mack Faragher (New York: Henry Holt, 1994), 158.

[2]Turner, *Rereading Frederick Jackson Turner*, 101. Latin American

historian Enrique Dussel argues that, as the first European to extend European civilization westward, Christopher Columbus was the first "modern" person. Modernity is defined by the need to conquer and subdue: "Columbus thus initiated modernity. . . . Because of his departure from Latin anti-Muslim Europe, the idea that the Occident was the center of history was inaugurated and came to pervade the European life world. Europe even projected its presumed centrality upon its own origins. Hence, Europeans thought either that Adam and Eve were Europeans or that their story portrayed the original myth of Europe to the exclusion of other cultures" (Dussel, *The Invention of the Americas: Eclipse of "the Other" and the Myth of Modernity* [New York: Continuum, 1995], 32).

[3]Turner, *Rereading Frederick Jackson Turner*, 32, 60.

[4]John Mack Faragher, Introduction, in ibid., 1.

[5]Turner, *Rereading Frederick Jackson Turner*, 96.

[6]Ray Allen Billington, *The Genesis of the Frontier Thesis: A Study in Historical Creativity* (San Marino, Calif.: Huntington Library, 1971), 72.

[7]Walter LaFeber, *Inevitable Revolutions: The United States in Central America* (New York: W. W. Norton, 1983), 300.

[8]Quoted in ibid., 33.

[9]Ibid., 35.

[10]Ibid., 36.

[11]Ibid., 39. The racist worldview underlying these statements is only too clear, especially when one compares U.S. attitudes toward immigration from Mexico with the very different attitudes toward immigration from Europe—at least white, Anglo-Saxon, Protestant Europe.

[12]Dussel, *Invention of the Americas*, 54. José de Acosta was more precise in his depiction of the indigenous peoples: "The third-class savages resemble wild animals. . . . There are infinite numbers of these in the New World. . . . For all those who are scarcely human or only half-human, it is fitting to teach them to be human and to instruct them as children. . . . One must also contain them by force . . . and even force them against their will (Luke 14:23) so that they might enter the kingdom of heaven" (quoted in ibid., 54). On the intimate connection between military and spiritual conquest, see also Luis N. Rivera, *A Violent Evangelism: The Political and Religious Conquest of the Americas* (Louisville, Ky.: Westminster/John Knox Press, 1992). That Latin America is still mission territory is reflected in the fact that, five centuries after Columbus, the majority of Catholic priests in Latin America are still foreign-born. And, of course, only a small minority of the priests ministering to the Latino/a community in the United States are native to that community.

[13]Fray Juan de Torquemada, quoted in Dussel, *Invention of the Americas*, 39.

[14]See Dussel, *Invention of the Americas*, 50-57.

[15]Charles H. Lippy, Robert Choquette, and Stafford Poole, *Christianity Comes to the Americas:1492-1776* (London: Paragon Press, 1992), 268.

[16]Forrest G. Wood, *The Arrogance of Faith: Christianity and Race in America from the Colonial Era to the Twentieth Century* (New York: Alfred A. Knopf, 1990), 221.

[17]Quoted in ibid., 35.

[18]Ibid., 35, 220.

[19]Ibid., 216-217. Martin Marty likewise notes the intimate connection between religious evangelization and military conquest for the English colonists: "The conquering Protestants regularly employed imperial language. As early as 1610 Virginia colonists were connecting missionary work with conquest and barter" (Marty, *Righteous Empire: The Protestant Experience in America* [New York: Dial Press, 1970], 5).

[20]Wood, *Arrogance of Faith*, 223.

[21]See, esp., Bartolomé de Las Casas, *The Devastation of the Indies: A Brief Account* (Baltimore: Johns Hopkins University Press, 1992), and Helen Parish, ed., *Bartolomé de Las Casas: The Only Way* (New York: Paulist Press, 1992). For a magisterial study of Las Casas's life and work, see Gustavo Gutiérrez, *Las Casas: In Search of the Poor of Jesus Christ* (Maryknoll, N.Y.: Orbis Books, 1993). Other critics of the conquest included Dominican friars Juan de Ramírez, Pedro de Córdoba, and Antonio de Montesinos, as well as Bishops Juan Fernández Angulo, Juan del Valle, and, especially, Antonio de Valdivieso. See Rivera, *Violent Evangelism*, 235-257; Enrique Dussel, *A History of the Church in Latin America: Colonialism to Liberation* (Grand Rapids: Eerdmans, 1981), 49-55.

[22]Marty, *Righteous Empire*, 8.

[23]Justo González, *Santa Biblia: The Bible through Hispanic Eyes* (Nashville: Abingdon, 1996), 85-86.

[24]Ibid.

[25]Ibid., 86. If one compares, for instance, the view of national borders represented by the North American Free Trade Agreement with that represented by recent anti-immigration laws, one receives a clear message: the United States will accord a freedom of movement to financial capital that it will not accord to mere human beings. The natural right of capital ("market forces," the "law" of supply and demand, "free" trade) to expand into new global markets must be affirmed as absolute and inviolable, while the right of labor (i.e., human beings) to do so must be artificially restricted.

²⁶Ibid., 86-87.

²⁷Such a recognition is not, moreover, a mere utopian ideal. As anyone who has lived in or traveled to Tijuana, El Paso, or Laredo knows, the actual reality of life on the border is very different from that portrayed in the frontier myth. In towns and cities all along the Rio Grande, a truly border culture is emerging in the shadows of the southern frontier's barbed-wire fences and stone walls: "Today, the borderlands between the U.S. and Mexico form the cradle of a new humanity. It is the meeting ground of ancient civilizations that have never met before. Old cultural borders are giving way and a new people is emerging. . . . The borders no longer mark the end limits of a country, a civilization, or even a hemisphere, but the starting points of a new space populated by a new human group" (Virgilio Elizondo, *The Future Is Mestizo: Life Where Cultures Meet* [Bloomington, Ind.: Meyer-Stone, 1988], x-xi).

²⁸This common Spanish word denoting persons who come from the United States would literally be translated as "United Statesans." In English, of course, no such word exists; "*estadounidenses*" are simply "Americans."

²⁹Douglas Edwards, "The Socio-Economic and Cultural Ethos of the Lower Galilee in the First Century: Implications for the Nascent Jesus Movement," in *The Galilee in Late Antiquity*, ed. Lee I. Levine (New York: Jewish Theological Seminary of America, 1992), 54.

³⁰Richard A. Horsley, *Galilee: History, Politics, People* (Valley Forge, Pa.: Trinity Press, 1995), 241.

³¹Jonathan Draper, "Jesus and the Renewal of Local Community in Galilee: Challenge to a Communitarian Christology," *Journal of Theology for Southern Africa* 87 (June 1994): 35-36.

³²Richard A. Horsley, *Archaeology, History, and Society in Galilee* (Valley Forge, Pa.: Trinity Press, 1996), 173.

³³Horsley, *Galilee*, 243-244.

³⁴Sean Freyne, "Galilee," in *The Oxford Companion to the Bible*, ed. Bruce M. Metzger and Michael David Coogan (New York: Oxford University Press, 1993), 242. See also Freyne's *Jesus: A Jewish Galilean* (New York: T & T Clark, 2004).

³⁵As I discuss in greater detail below with regard to Elizondo's work, it is important to distinguish between a racial-ethnic interpretation and a theological interpretation of Galilee, since the former has a tragic history in Western intellectual and political circles. In other words, I am in no way denying that Galilee was thoroughly Jewish ethnically; what I am suggesting is that its proximity to and history of domination by Roman and Hellenistic cultures (i.e., its character as a borderland) became theologically and soteriologically identified with what Freyne describes

as "the newness of Jesus' vision," a newness that—like most newness—was perceived as dangerous and threatening by the centers of power, whether Roman or Jewish.

[36]Michael E. Lee, "*Galilean Journey* Revisited: Mestizaje, Anti-Judaism, and the Dynamic of Exclusion," *Theological Studies* (forthcoming).

[37]See especially Jean-Pierre Ruiz, "Good Fences and Good Neighbors? Biblical Scholars and Theologians," *Journal of Hispanic/Latino Theology* (May 2007), available at www.latinotheology.org, and Jeffrey S. Siker, "Historicizing a Racialized Jesus: Case Studies in the 'Black Christ,' the 'Mestizo Christ,' and White Critique," *Biblical Interpretation* 15 (2007), 26-53.

[38]Clodomiro L. Siller Acuña, *Para comprender el mensaje de María de Guadalupe* (Buenos Aires: Editorial Guadalupe, 1989), 58. Siller provides the complete text of the story with a commentary. It is important to note that some scholars have raised serious questions about the origins of the Guadalupan narrative, e.g., Stafford Poole, *Our Lady of Guadalupe: The Origins and Sources of a Mexican National Symbol, 1531-1797* (Tucson: University of Arizona Press, 1995). Other scholars have, in turn, raised methodological questions about these revisionist critiques themselves, e.g., Richard Nebel, *Santa María Tonantzin, Virgen de Guadalupe: Continuidad y transformación religiosa en México* (Mexico City: Fondo de Cultura Económica, 1995). A systematic analysis of this debate is beyond the scope of this paper. My concern here is to analyze the explicit content of the narrative itself. Thus, for example, I assume the narrative's identification of *La Morenita* with Mary (though with clear allusions to Tonantzin). A provocative, alternative interpretation is being developed by Orlando Espín, who suggests that, in the light of popular practice, the Marian language might perhaps be better understood in pneumatological categories; see Orlando Espín, *The Faith of the People: Theological Reflections on Popular Catholicism* (Maryknoll, N.Y.: Orbis Books, 1997), 8-10.

[39]For accounts and interpretations of the Guadalupan narrative, see esp. the following works: Clodomiro L. Siller Acuña, "Anotaciones y comentarios al *Nican Mopohua*," *Estudios Indígenas* 8, no. 2 (1981): 217-274; Siller Acuña, *Flor y canto del Tepeyac: Historia de las apariciones de Santa María de Guadalupe, texto y comentario* (Xalapa, Veracruz, México: Servir, 1981); Siller Acuña, *Para comprender el mensaje de María de Guadalupe* (Buenos Aires: Editorial Guadalupe, 1989); Jacques Lafaye, *Quetzalcóatl and Guadalupe: The Formation of Mexican National Consciousness, 1531-1813* (Chicago: University of Chicago Press, 1976); Virgilio Elizondo, *La Morenita: Evangelizer*

of the Americas (San Antonio, Tex.: Mexican American Cultural Center, 1980); Virgilio Elizondo, *Guadalupe: Mother of the New Creation* (Maryknoll, N.Y.; Orbis Books, 1997); Nebel, *Santa María Tonantzin*; Poole, *Our Lady of Guadalupe*; Jeanette Rodríguez, *Our Lady of Guadalupe: Faith and Empowerment among Mexican American Women* (Austin: University of Texas Press, 1994).

[40]See Elizondo, *Guadalupe*, ix-xx.

[41]Elizondo, *La Morenita*, 83; Rodríguez, *Our Lady of Guadalupe*, 22-30; Orlando O. Espín, "Tradition and Popular Religion: An Understanding of the *Sensus Fidelium*," in *Frontiers of Hispanic Theology in the United States*, ed. Alan Figueroa Deck (Maryknoll, N.Y.: Orbis Books, 1992), 72-75.

[42]Rodríguez, *Our Lady of Guadalupe*, 27.

[43]David Tracy, *The Analogical Imagination: Christian Theology and the Culture of Pluralism* (New York: Crossroad, 1981), xi.

[44]Enrique Dussel, *Ética de la Liberación: En la Edad de la Globalización y de la Exclusión* (Madrid: Editorial Trotta, 1998), 68. (This and all subsequent translations from the book are my translation.)

[45]Dussel, *Invention of the Americas*, 17.

[46]Dussel, *Ética de la Liberación*, 61-62.

[47]Ibid., 77.

[48]Enrique Dussel, "The Bread of the Eucharistic Celebration as a Sign of Justice in the Community," in *Can We Always Celebrate the Eucharist?* ed. Mary Collins and David Power (New York: Seabury, 1982), 56-65.

[49]Ibid., 60-62.

[50]This text is quoted in the brilliant, inspiring work on the life and thought of Las Casas written by Gutiérrez, *Las Casas*, 47.

[51]Ibid., 46-61.

[52]One should note the tragic irony, however, that Las Casas did not condemn the practice of African slavery until the end of his life, initially seeing this as an alternative to the enslavement of the Amerindians.

[53]Gutiérrez, *Las Casas*, 154-189.

[54]Dussel, *Ética de la Liberación*, 202-206.

[55]Ibid., 91. Here I would concur with those Latino and Latina scholars who warn of the risks implicit in an "aesthetic turn" inattentive to the crucial importance of economic justice. (See, esp., Manuel C. Mejido, "A Critique of the 'Aesthetic Turn' in U.S. Hispanic Theology: A Dialogue with Roberto Goizueta and the Positing of a New Paradigm," *Journal of Hispanic/Latino Theology* 8, no. 3 [2001]: 18-48.) Indeed, over the years I myself have repeatedly warned of that danger and, therefore, have argued for the crucial importance of economic justice as the

necessary mediation of any aesthetics. That concern, for instance, is at the heart of my critique of José Vasconcelos's aesthetics and Balthasar's own theological aesthetics. See, e.g., the section subtitled "The Insufficiency of Aesthetics" in my *Caminemos con Jesús: Toward a Hispanic/Latino Theology of Accompaniment* (Maryknoll, N.Y.: Orbis Books, 1994), 119-131.

[56]Dussel, *Ética de la Liberación*, 17.

[57]Ibid., 524.

[58]Ibid., 559.

[59]Ibid., 137-138.

[60]"The quest for human purity," contends Virgilio Elizondo, "defines boundaries and very quickly excludes those who have been the product of territorial transgression. There seems to be an inner fear that the children of territorial transgression pose the deepest threat to the existence of the group and to the survival of its purity" (*Future Is Mestizo*, 80).

Index